Crochet for Children

Crochet for Children

Get your kids hooked
on crochet with these
35 simple projects
to make together

Claire Montgomerie

CICO BOOKS
LONDON NEW YORK

Published in 2011 by CICO Books
an imprint of Ryland Peters & Small Ltd
519 Broadway, 5th Floor, New York, NY 10012

www.cicobooks.com

10 9 8 7 6 5 4 3 2 1

A CIP catalog record for this book is available
from the Library of Congress.

ISBN: 978 1 907563 81 2

Printed in China

Editor: Kate Haxell
Design: Emma and Tom Forge
Photography: Martin Norris
Additional photography: Emma Mitchell
Styling: Sophie Martell

Contents

Introduction

Crochet is a craft that is often considered the poor cousin of knitting and so often is—I think wrongly—forgotten or dismissed as old-fashioned or not relevant. However, crochet stitches are much easier to work in the round and in three-dimensions than knitting, which makes it the perfect craft for toy-making, and so I think is a great skill for children to pick up. Aside from this, there are many other practical reasons to learn to crochet, especially as a child. It is a fun pastime, but it could also be beneficial to children's development. Crocheting involves a lot of counting and simple maths, as well as being relaxing and therapeutic, which means that it can aid learning and concentration in some children, especially in those with learning difficulties or attention disorders.

The main problem is that there are far fewer crochet books than those that champion knitting, and it is even harder to find a crochet book that caters for children. It is imperative that a child has a book aimed at their age group as, through teaching many groups of both adults and children how to crochet and knit, I have discovered that the methods needed to teach both groups are very different.

It is important that, while a child-friendly book should not be too complicated, it should also not be too simple or babyish. The projects must be interesting enough to hold a child's interest, as their concentration span can be very short, though they can most definitely cope with more challenging patterns. Bearing this in mind, I have aimed to write an interesting, informative, and fun book, with lots of simple yet alluringly colorful patterns, which are both exciting and easy to make. I also wanted the projects to be modern and fresh, to prove that crochet is most definitely not an old-fashioned craft—and have even used the traditional, and often derided, granny square in new and interesting ways.

I believe that anyone can learn to crochet; all it takes is lots of practice and perseverance, which we know not all children want to do. However, the projects in this book are so small, simple, and repetitive that I hope they will want to move onto the next, and will not even realize that they are progressing through the techniques. The toys mainly use similar techniques in a basic body, with non-crocheted embellishment. So that once a child is used to the technique involved, they can choose the shape they like and finish their toy with felt, fabric, beads, and buttons in whichever way they wish to create their own unique creatures and animals, encouraging individuality and creativity.

With the yarn, I have tried to choose compositions that are easy to use and often formulated especially for children, utilizing a mix of natural fibers to ensure they are kind to young, sensitive skin, and manmade fibers to make them durable and easy to wash and care for. However, I have also suggested alternatives so you and your child can play with the look of the projects and use remnants of yarns that are to hand, as many of the patterns use very small amounts of yarn. People mistakenly often think that crochet projects can only use crochet cotton. The trouble with this material is that is can be hard and very fine, which is not conducive to a fun and quick-to-work project, so I have introduced lots of wools and other fibers as well, which should be kind to your child's hands and be easy to hold.

Before you dive into the patterns, please do take the time to read my tips on teaching your child to crochet (see page 8), as I hope my hints and tricks will help make the experience enjoyable and ensure the memory is a warm and happy one for all involved. Most importantly of all, don't forget to have fun!

Claire Montgomerie

Teaching kids to crochet

While teaching all kinds of craft workshops for children, I have developed a few priceless and failsafe practices, which should ensure that crochet will become a fun hobby for any young child. Even if you do not follow them all rigidly, I recommend you stick at least to the simple tools and materials and have a play with the techniques and tips to find out what your child enjoys crocheting.

Your first question is probably, what is the best age to begin teaching your child how to crochet? The truth is, there is no perfect age, as it depends on the individual. It is possible to learn the very basics as young as four or five, if your child has highly developed motor skills and is used to doing arts and crafts with you. However, I have found that the best age is seven or eight, as by this time most children are dexterous enough, have good hand-eye coordination, and can concentrate for longer periods of time. They will also be more likely to take all the techniques in and adopt crochet as a hobby and skill that they never forget.

Crochet can be fiddly to learn, due to the need to hold the yarn correctly, so to gauge whether you think your child may be ready to learn, the best thing to do is to teach them to create long lengths of chain. The basic crochet stitches can be quite tricky to master at first and are nearly impossible if you have not first perfected the trick of holding the yarn to create an even gauge. The good news is that once the gauge is mastered, the stitches can be picked up very quickly, as each stitch builds upon the last. So encourage your child to practice getting the perfect gauge by making long lengths of basic chain until you feel that they are ready to move onto the stitches. The chains can easily be made into necklaces or friendship bracelets so that your child doesn't feel as though making them is a fruitless activity.

When choosing tools and materials, there are a few pointers to follow to make them more desirable to young fingers. Metal or metal-tipped hooks are the best kind to use, as the shank is smooth and slippery and the hook is well defined, which means the yarn will slip over the tip more easily and stitches will not snag as much. If you look around, you can find brightly colored hooks, or sparkly ones, which should make them instantly desirable to the young eye. It is also best to work on projects

that use medium-thickness hooks, of around US D/3–H/8 (3–5mm), so that children are not working with stitches that are too small and intricate, or with hooks that are too unwieldy.

Traditionally cotton is assumed to be the only fiber for crochet. However, any yarn can be used, so long as it is smooth and not a fancy yarn, such as a bouclé. In fact, for the first project a traditional crochet thread can be a bit thin, hard, and uncomfortable to use, so it is probably best to use a smooth and stretchy, relatively cheap yarn, such as wool or acrylic, as this will be easier on the child's hands and the project will "grow" more quickly.

Go slowly with your child at first, they are generally happy just playing with the yarn and techniques—make the learning like a game. Try to vary the activity as you teach, so have pompom makers and sewing needles to hand to embellish the fabric and break up the monotony of the crochet stitches, especially when you notice any concentration lapses. Don't make them crochet for too long, especially at first. It is a repetitive skill, which can cause unpracticed hands to ache. Short, fun lessons with breaks will stop children feeling that they are being forced to crochet and will make them look forward to picking up the hook again. You do not have to practice every day, so long as you crochet regularly. Perhaps you can find time to crochet during a favorite cartoon or before bedtime to unwind. Maybe Saturday evenings will be craft time. Any regular quality time with mom, dad, or grandma will be eagerly anticipated and if you include all your children in some way, and even their friends, they will want to do it more as it will be something they can share and talk about.

Have patience with your child; it seems patronizing to say so, but sometimes after a long day together, a parent can often be less patient with his or her own child, especially if they really want the child to share in the love of something dear to them. Even if a terrible mess is occurring, try not rip back a child's work too far, which can undermine their confidence in their ability—let them see their progression from wonky fabrics with sloping sides to beautiful, even crochet.

The best tip I can give you is: make it fun! While an adult will happily crochet large projects, children want to see results quickly or they may get bored or lose concentration. Small projects such as a belt or toy—or those that are made up of motifs such as granny squares—are preferable to the failsafe adult beginner project, the scarf. Crochet should always be relaxing and fun, otherwise what's the point? So ensure you both enjoy the process and do not put too much emphasis on perfectly finished fabrics. Be flexible and encourage your child to use their imagination; projects can evolve as they are made, developing into a final piece dictated by the shape of the fabric. Every child is different and they have a very different view of the world to adults, so let them form fabulous creations from their fabrics, and perhaps in return they can teach you a thing or two about crochet!

Techniques

Tools

You need just two items to start crocheting: a hook and some yarn. However, there are a few other bits and pieces that you'll need to make some of the projects in this book, but none of them are expensive and you'll probably have some of them at home already.

▲ **Crochet hook** Hooks come in different materials and sizes. Each pattern tells you the size you'll need to make the project.

▼ **Beads** These are great for adding extra decoration or sparkle to a project. Just sew them on when the crochet is complete.

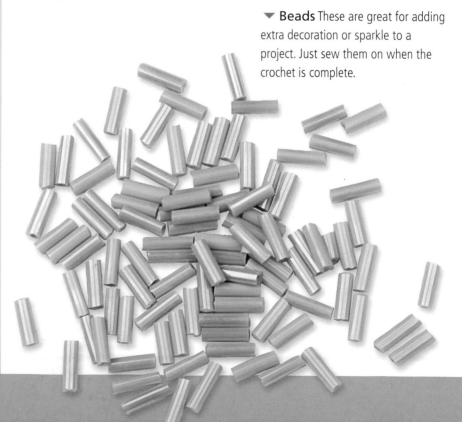

▲ **Pompom maker** These little gadgets offer a quick and easy way to make pompom embellishments.

▲ **Stitch marker** Markers are used, especially in rounds, where you need to keep track of the beginning of a row or a certain point in your crochet.

▲ **Buttons** Another way of adding color and decoration, buttons are especially good as eyes for toys.

▼ **Scissors** Always cut your yarn, don't break it, even when the pattern says "break yarn."

◀ **Sewing needle and thread** You'll need these to sew decorations and felt additions to your projects.

Holding the hook

There are two ways of holding the hook in crochet, and you can choose whichever of these feels most natural for you.

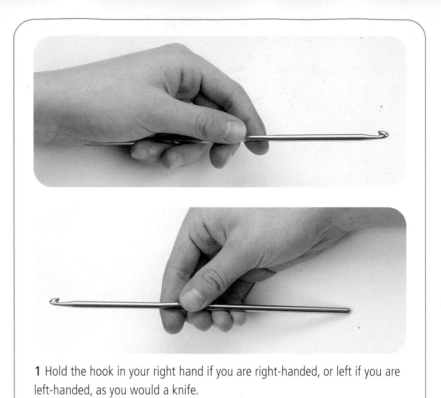

1 Hold the hook in your right hand if you are right-handed, or left if you are left-handed, as you would a knife.

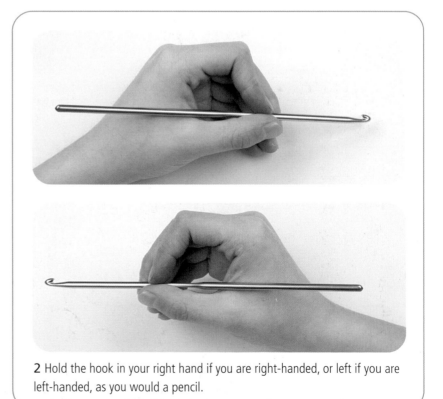

2 Hold the hook in your right hand if you are right-handed, or left if you are left-handed, as you would a pencil.

Holding the yarn

Creating the correct, even gauge is imperative in crochet, otherwise the stitches are nearly impossible to create. This is achieved by how you wrap the yarn around your fingers.

RIGHT-HANDED

1 Wrap the ball end of the yarn around little finger of your left hand, passing it over the other fingers.

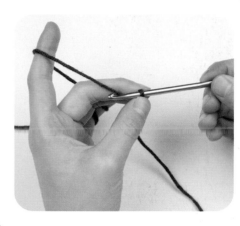

2 Hold the hook in your right hand. Hold the work steady (here, the bottom of the slip knot is being held), with the middle finger and thumb of your left hand, then use your left forefinger to create tension by keeping it held above the work.

LEFT-HANDED

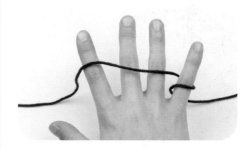

1 Wrap the ball end of the yarn around little finger of your right hand, passing it over the other fingers.

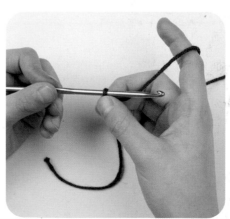

2 Hold the hook in your left hand. Hold the work steady (here, the bottom of the slip knot is being held), with the middle finger and thumb of your right hand, then use your right forefinger to create tension by keeping it held above the work.

Slip knot

The first loop on the hook in crochet is created by a slip knot.

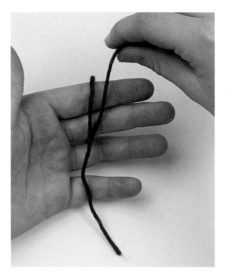

1 Make a loop of the yarn around your fingers.

2 Pull a second loop of yarn through the first loop.

3 Pull up the loop, but do not pull the end of yarn through.

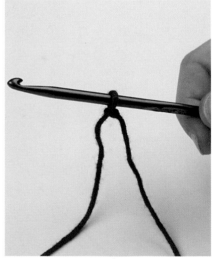

4 Slip the hook through the second loop and pull the loop taut around the hook. Do not pull too tightly or the first chain will be hard to make.

Chain

Most crochet projects begin with a length of chain. This is the perfect stitch to practice your gauge on, as it is the simplest thing you can do in crochet.

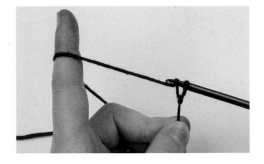

2 Turn the hook around toward you to catch the yarn and pull a loop through the loop on the hook.

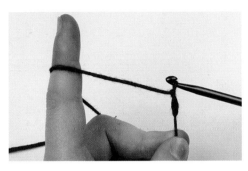

3 One chain is made.

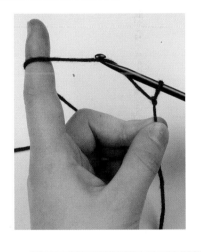

1 Holding the yarn and hook in the appropriate hands, hold the tail end of the yarn under the slip knot and bring the working yarn over the hook by passing the hook in front of yarn then under it: this is called "yarn over" and will be referred to that way for the rest of these technique instructions.

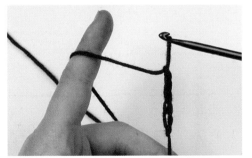

4 Ensuring the stitches are even—not too loose or tight—repeat Step 2 to make a length of chain.

WORKING INTO A CHAIN

You might need to concentrate a bit more when making stitches into a chain, but once you have done the first row, it's much easier to continue.

1 You need to miss the appropriate number of chain for your particular stitch (see the individual stitch instructions), then insert the hook from front to back into the next chain, under the top loop of the chain.

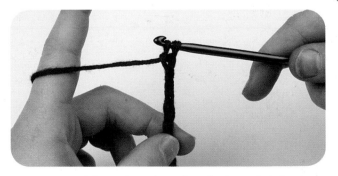

2 Yarn over and draw a loop through to the front of chain, then complete the stitch. (See pages 18–23 for stitch instructions.)

Single crochet (sc)

This is the next crochet stitch to learn once you have got chain right.

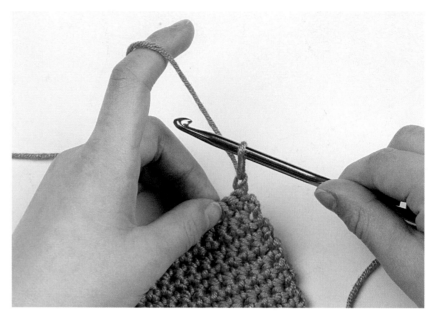

1 Make one chain (see page 17). This is called the "turning chain" and you make one at the start of every row of single crochet.

2 Skipping the chain you have just made, insert the hook from front to back into the next stitch (see page 24). There should be the two strands of the stitch and one loop on the hook.

3 Yarn over hook.

4 Draw the loop through the stitch to the front. There should be two loops on the hook.

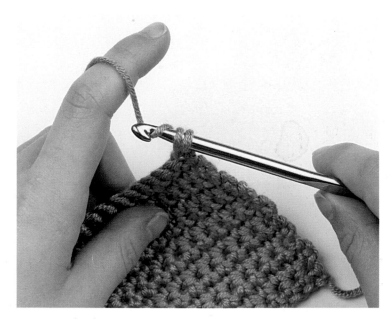

5 Yarn over hook again.

6 Draw the loop through both loops on the hook to complete one single crochet. Follow Steps 2–6 to work one single crochet in the same way into every stitch across the row.

Half double crochet (hdc)

This stitch involves a third loop on the hook. You need to work two chain (see page 17) for the turning chain at the start of a row of half double crochet.

1 Yarn over hook before you insert the hook into the next stitch.

2 Insert the hook in the next stitch, from front to back (see page 24). Yarn over hook.

3 Pull the loop through the stitch only. There should be three loops on the hook.

4 Yarn over hook again.

5 Pull the loop through the three loops on the hook to complete one half double crochet. Work one half double crochet in the same way into every stitch across the row.

Double crochet (dc)

This is the last crochet stitch to learn in the series of stitches you need to know for this book.

1 Work three chain (see page 17) for the turning chain at the start of a row of double crochet.

2 Yarn over hook before you insert the hook into the stitch.

3 Insert the hook into the next stitch, from front to back (see page 24). Yarn over hook.

4 Draw the loop just through the stitch. There should be three loops on the hook.

5 Yarn over hook.

6 Pull the loop through two of the loops on the hook. There should be two loops on the hook.

7 Yarn over hook.

8 Pull the loop through the remaining two loops on the hook to complete a double crochet. Follow Steps 2–8 to work one double crochet in the same way into every stitch across the row.

Fasten off

When you have finished crocheting, you need to fasten off the stitches to stop all your work unraveling.

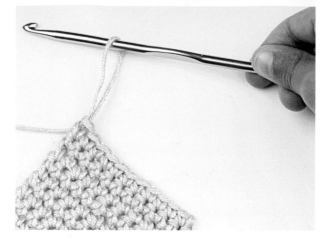

1 Pull up the final loop of the last stitch to make it bigger.

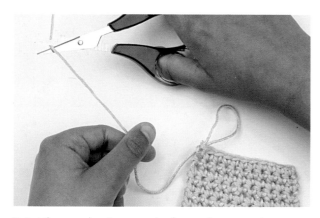

2 Cut the yarn, leaving enough of an end to weave in.

3 Pull the end through the loop.

4 Pull the loop up tightly.

WORKING INTO WHICH LOOP?

All crochet stitches are always worked through both loops of the next stitch (looks like a "V" on top of the stitch), unless the pattern tells you otherwise. Insert the hook under both loops of the next stitch, then complete the stitch.

In this book, you are sometimes asked to work through the back loop only (blo) to create texture. Insert the hook under the back loop only of the next stitch, going through the center of the stitch to the back, then complete the stitch.

Slip stitch

A slip stitch is usually used to join one stitch to another, or to join a stitch to another point. It is most often used in this book when joining a round, as here.

1 Work until you have reached the end of the round.

2 Insert hook into next stitch; here it is the first stitch of the last round.

3 Yarn over hook, as when you make a chain (see page 17).

4 Pull a loop through every loop on hook to finish the slip stitch and close the round.

Increasing

To work an extra stitch, you simply need to work into the same stitch more than once. The method is shown here on single crochet (see page 18).

1 Work one stitch as normal.

2 Insert the hook once again into the stitch you just worked into and work a second stitch.

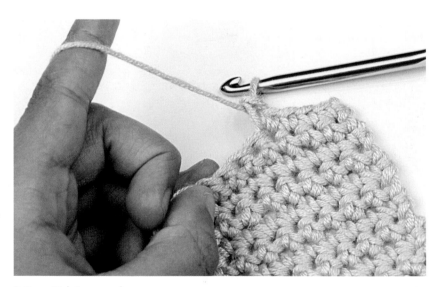

3 One stitch increased.

Decreasing

To decrease a stitch, you need to work into two stitches without finishing them, then work them together. Here, a single crochet (see page 18) decrease is worked to demonstrate the method.

2 Draw a loop through the stitch, but do not finish the single crochet stitch as usual.

3 Insert the hook into the next stitch. Yarn over hook.

1 Insert the hook into the next stitch. Yarn over hook.

4 Draw the loop through the stitch only, there should be three loops on hook in total. Yarn over hook.

5 Draw the loop through all the loops on the hook, drawing two stitches together. One stitch decreased.

Working in the round

There are a few ways to work in the round, and here we show you the two ways used in this book. Method 1 creates a hole in the middle of the work, which can be part of a decorative design. Method 2 creates a center with a smaller hole, perfect for toys.

METHOD 1

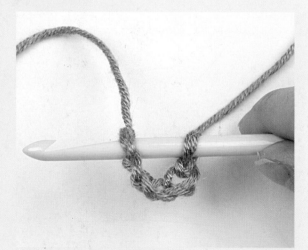

1 Work chain (see page 17) to the length given in the pattern. Insert the hook through the first chain made to create a horseshoe shape.

2 Work a slip stitch (see page 25) to join the horseshoe into a ring.

4 Pull a loop through the center of the ring to the front. Two loops are on the hook. Yarn over hook and pull the loop through the two loops on the hook to complete a single crochet. Work the desired number of stitches into the ring in the same way.

3 You can now continue working into this ring as you wish. Here, a series of single crochet stitches (see page 18) are worked around the ring. Insert the hook into the center of the ring. Yarn over hook.

5 Join the round with a slip stitch to the first single crochet made (see page 25). First round is complete.

METHOD 2

1 Work two chain stitches (see page 17).

2 Insert the hook into the first chain made.

3 Work a single crochet into this chain, then work as many single crochets as needed into the same chain.

4 Join the round with a slip stitch to the first single crochet made (see page 25). First round is complete.

Joining in a new color

Sometimes you will need to change yarn color, but it's very easy to do.

2 Insert the hook into the stitch at the beginning of the next row, then insert the hook through the slip knot.

3 Pull the loop of the slip knot through to the front of the fabric.

1 Fasten off the old color (see page 24). Make a slip knot with the new color (see page 16).

4 Yarn round hook.

5 Work one chain (see page 17) to hold in the new color, then complete the first stitch as normal.

Sewing up

Sewing up crochet fabric can be done in many ways, but using a whip stitch is the easiest. However, you can see it quite easily so you can make a feature of it by using a different color yarn to the one used in the project.

Lay the two pieces to be joined next to each other with right sides upward. Secure the yarn to one piece. Insert the needle into the front of one piece of fabric, then up from the back of the adjoining fabric. Repeat along the seam.

Sewing crochet to fabric

There are a few projects in this book where you need to sew some crochet to a piece of fabric. As with sewing up two crochet pieces, you use whip stitch.

Use a sewing needle and thread. Wrong sides facing, lay the two pieces to be joined on top of each other. Insert the needle from the back and bring it through to the front. Repeat along the seam.

Pompoms

Pompoms are so simple to make. You can make them from rings of cardboard, but buying a plastic pompom maker is so much quicker and simpler and you don't have to make a new one each time you want to make pompoms. You can buy them in all shapes and sizes—even heart-shaped! Here is a little tip: try cutting the yarn for tying before you begin so you don't have to put down the pompom maker in the middle of cutting the pompom.

1 Wind yarn around each half of the pompom maker.

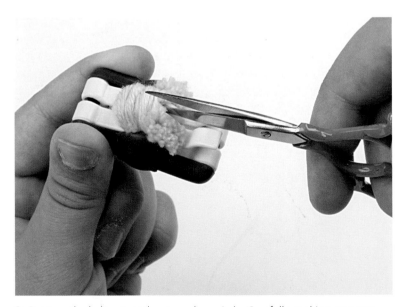

2 Put two the halves together to make a circle. Carefully, making sure you don't lose any ends, cut around the outside of the circle.

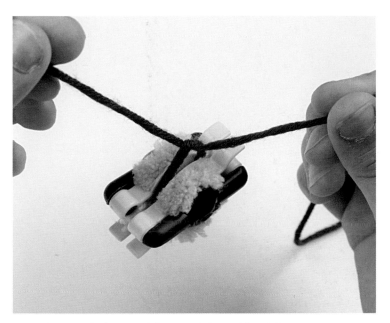

3 Tie a loose end of yarn tightly around the middle of the pompom. Try to wrap around another time and tie a knot again to ensure the pompom is tied securely.

4 Pull the pompom maker apart to create the pompom.

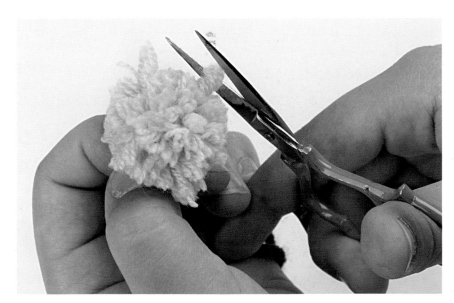

5 Trim any straggly ends of yarn to make a neat ball.

Chapter 2

Warm and Cozy

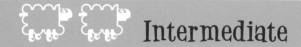 **Intermediate**

Rabbit Scarf

A very basic pattern made fun to wear by adding a pompom tail and floppy ears to create a cute bunny scarf!

MEASUREMENTS

One size—you can customize the length to fit you, but the scarf is approx 5½in (14cm) wide.

YARN

1 x 3½oz (100g) ball—approx 246yds (225m)—Artesano Silk Embrace, 47% Suri Alpaca, 53% silk, in shade 10, tango white

ALTERNATIVE YARNS

Any heavy Aran or worsted or chunky weight yarn will do, furry or not. For a first project, it is preferable to try a smooth yarn for ease of crocheting. You can also use different thickness yarns and change your hook to match, the scarf will just come out bigger or smaller!

GAUGE (TENSION)

Exact gauge isn't essential, but 15 sts and 8 rows to 4in (10cm) in hdc using size K/10.5 (6.5mm) hook or size required to obtain correct gauge.

NOTIONS

∗Size K/10.5 (6.5mm) crochet hook
∗Two buttons for eyes
∗Felt for cheeks and teeth or other features
∗Darning needle
∗Sewing needle and thread

SCARF

Using size K/10.5 (6.5mm) hook, ch 9.

Row 1: Work 1hdc into 3rd ch from hook, work 1hdc into each ch to end of row. *7hdc*

Row 2: Ch 2, work 1hdc into same st, 5hdc, work 2hdc into last st. *9hdc*

Row 3: Ch 2, work 1hdc into same st, 7hdc, work 2hdc into last st. *11hdc*

Row 4: Ch 2, work 1hdc into same st, 9hdc, work 2hdc into last st. *13hdc*

Row 5: Ch 2, work 1hdc into same st, 11hdc, work 2hdc into last st. *15hdc*

Work even in hdc on these 15 sts until scarf measures approx 47in (120cm) or desired length.

Next row: Ch 2, skip next st, 11hdc, skip next st, hdc into last st. *13hdc*

Next row: Ch 2, skip next st, 9hdc, skip next st, hdc into last st. *11hdc*

Next row: Ch 2, skip next st, 7hdc, skip next st, hdc into last st. *9hdc*

Next row: Ch 2, skip next st, 5hdc, skip next st, hdc into last st. *7hdc*

Fasten off yarn.

EAR

(make two)

Work ch 2, then work 2hdc into first ch.

Row 1: Ch 2, work 1hdc into same st, 1hdc, work 2hdc into last st. *5hdc*

Work even in hdc for ten rows.

Next row: Ch 2, skip next st, hdc, skip next st, hdc into last st. *3hdc*

Fasten off yarn.

FINISHING

Sew ears to face end of scarf.

Sew buttons to head for eyes.

Cut pieces of felt for teeth and nose and sew to face.

Make pompom of approx 2½in (6cm) in diameter and sew to back end.

 **Easy**

Fingerless Gloves

You may think gloves are hard to crochet, but these are simply two rectangles sewn along one side, with a gap left for the thumb!

MEASUREMENTS

Short gloves approx 4½in (11.5cm) long.
Long gloves approx 6in (15cm) long.
Both lengths to fit S(L) approx 6¼(7)in [16(18)cm] around hand.

YARN

1 x 1¾oz (50g) ball—approx 120yds (112m)—of Artesano Soft Merino Superwash DK, 100% merino superwash, in each of:
Short gloves
Yarn A: shade 6315, lime green
Yarn B: shade 1291, sea blue
Long gloves
Yarn A: shade SFN10, cream
Yarn B: shade 8413, baby peach

ALTERNATIVE YARNS

Any DK or light worsted weight yarn will do; try plain colors or different width stripes to play with the pattern.

GAUGE (TENSION)

Approx 16 sts and 13 rows to 4in (10cm) in hdc using size 7 (4.5mm) hook or size required to obtain correct gauge.

NOTIONS

*Size 7 (4.5mm) crochet hook
*Darning needle
*Three buttons (for long gloves)
*Sewing needle and thread

SHORT GLOVES

(make 2)

Using size 7 (4.5mm) hook and yarn A, ch 28(32).

Row 1: Work 1hdc into 2nd ch from hook, work 1hdc into each ch to end. *26(30)sts*

*Fasten off yarn A.

In yarn B, work even in hdc for 3 rows.

Fasten off yarn B.

Work 1 row even in hdc in yarn A; rep from * until glove measures 4½in (11.5cm) long, ending with 1 row of yarn A.

FINISHING

Sew up side seam to 1¼in (3cm) from top of glove and 1in (2.5cm) from bottom of glove, leaving a gap of 1½in (4cm) for thumb.

LONG GLOVES

(make 2)

Using size 7 (4.5mm) hook and yarn A, ch 28(32).

Row 1: Work 1hdc into 2nd ch from hook, work 1hdc into each ch to end. *26(30)sts*

*Fasten off yarn A.

In yarn B, work even in hdc for 1 row.

Fasten off yarn B.

Work 1 row even in hdc in yarn A; rep from * until glove measures 6in (15cm) long, ending with 1 row of yarn A.

FINISHING
Sew up side seam to 1½in (4cm) from top of glove and 3in (7.5cm) from bottom of glove, leaving a gap of 1½in (4cm) for thumb. Sew three buttons to wrist on opposite side to thumb hole.

Easy

Beanie Hat

A very cute and simple beanie hat, which will work up in no time at all in the easiest of stitches. You can make it more fun by adding funny animal ears and a face, or just wear it plain and simple!

MEASUREMENTS
S[M:L]
Finished hat approx 19(21:22½)in [48(52.5:57)cm] unstretched.

YARN
1 x 3½oz (100g) ball—approx 218yds (200m)—Rico Essentials Soft Merino Aran, 100% merino superwash, in each of:
Yarn A: shade 81, fawn
Yarn B: shade 15, violet (only very small quantities used)

ALTERNATIVE YARNS
Any Aran or worsted weight yarn will do here. The ears use very small amounts of yarn so you could use a contrasting scrap yarn left over from another project of any weight you wish, because the ears do not need to be the same size as the ones pictured.

GAUGE (TENSION)
17 sts and 21 rows to 4in (10cm) in sc in the round using a size 7 (4.5mm) hook or size required to obtain correct gauge.

NOTIONS
∗Size 7 (4.5mm) crochet hook
∗Darning needle
∗Felt for features
∗Sewing needle and thread
∗Two buttons for eyes

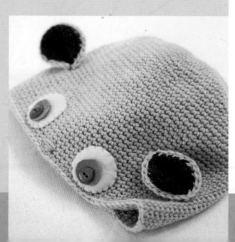

HAT
Using size 7 (4.5mm) hook and yarn A, ch 2.

Rnd 1: Work 6sc into first ch, join into round with a ss.

Rnd 2: Ch 1, work 2sc into each st around join rnd with a ss. *12sc*

Rnd 3: Ch 1, (1sc, work 2sc into next st) around, join rnd with a ss. *18sc*

Rnd 4: Ch 1, (2sc, work 2sc into next st) around, join rnd with a ss. *24sc*

Rnd 5: Ch 1, (3sc, work 2sc into next st) around, join rnd with a ss. *30sc*

Rnd 6: Ch 1, (4sc, work 2sc into next st) around, join rnd with a ss. *36sc*

Rnd 7: Ch 1, (5sc, work 2sc into next st) around, join rnd with a ss. *42sc*

Rnd 8: Ch 1, (6sc, work 2sc into next st) around, join rnd with a ss. *48sc*

Rnd 9: Ch 1, (7sc, work 2sc into next st) around, join rnd with a ss. *54sc*

Rnd 10: Ch 1, (8sc, work 2sc into next st) around, join rnd with a ss. *60sc*

Work 1 rnd even.

Rnd 12: Ch 1, (9sc, work 2sc into next st) around, join rnd with a ss. *66sc*

Work 1 rnd even.

Rnd 14: Ch 1, (10sc, work 2sc into next st) around, join rnd with a ss. *72sc*

Work 1 rnd even.

Rnd 16: Ch 1, (11sc, work 2sc into next st) around, join rnd with a ss. *78sc*

M and L sizes only:

Work 1 rnd even.

Rnd 18: Ch 1, (12sc, work 2sc into next st) around, join rnd with a ss. *84sc*

Work 1 rnd even.

Rnd 20: Ch 1, (13sc, work 2sc into next st) around, join rnd with a ss. *90sc*

L size only:

Work 1 rnd even.

Rnd 22: Ch 1, (14sc, work 2sc into next st) around, join rnd with a ss. *96sc*

All sizes:

Work even in sc for a further 4¾(5:5½in) [12(13:14)cm].

Fasten off yarn.

EARS

(make 2)

Using size 7 (4.5mm) hook and yarn A, ch 2.

Row 1: Work 4sc into first ch, turn.

Row 2: Ch 1, work 2sc into each st across row, turn. *8sc*

Row 3: Ch 1, (1sc, work 2sc into next st) across row, turn. *12sc*

Row 4: Ch 1, (2sc, work 2sc into next st) across row, turn. *16sc*

Row 5: Ch 1, (3sc, work 2sc into next st) across row, turn. *20sc*

Row 6: Ch 1, (4sc, work 2sc into next st) across row. *24sc*

Fasten off yarn.

Using size 7 (4.5mm) hook and yarn B, ch 2.

Row 1: Work 4sc into first ch, turn.

Row 2: Ch 1, work 2sc into each st across row, turn. *8sc*

Row 3: Ch 1, (1sc, work 2sc into next st) across row, turn. *12sc*

Row 4: Ch 1, (2sc, work 2sc into next st) across row, turn. *16sc*

Row 5: Ch 1, (3sc, work 2sc into next st) across row. *20sc*

Fasten off yarn.

FINISHING

Sew smaller ear piece onto larger ear piece.

Fold ear along straight seam, sew up and sew to side of hat.

Cut eyes from felt and sew them to the front of the hat. Sew buttons onto the felt to finish the eyes.

Using a scrap of yarn, embroider a triangular nose.

Advanced

Mittens

Warm and snug mittens made using a yarn that changes color throughout, so you don't even need to crochet stripes!

MEASUREMENTS
S(M:L), approx 5½(6½:7¼)in [14(16.5:18.5)cm] long. 5½(8½:8½)in [14(21.5:21.5)cm] around hand.

YARN
1(2:2) x 1¾oz (50g) ball—approx 190yds (174m)—Crystal Palace Yarns, Mochi Plus, 80% merino wool, 20% nylon, in shade 551, intense rainbow

ALTERNATIVE YARNS
Any Aran or worsted weight yarn will do, and you can stripe up different shades if you cannot find a variegated yarn that stripes itself. Wool or a wool-mix yarn is great for warmth.

GAUGE (TENSION)
Approx 17 sts and 20 rows to 4in (10cm) over sc using size H/8 (5mm) hook or size required to obtain correct gauge.

NOTIONS
∗Size H/8 (5mm) and size 7 (4.5mm) crochet hooks
∗Darning needle

PATTERN NOTES
Mittens are worked in the round, do not turn throughout. Rounds worked in spirals—do not join rounds. Place a marker in first stitch of round to mark beginning of rounds and count rounds, moving marker up every round.

MITTENS
(make 2)

Using size H/8 (5mm) hook, ch 2.

Rnd 1: Work 6sc into first ch made, do not join rnd.

Rnd 2: Work 2sc into each sc around. *12sc*

Rnd 3: (Work 2sc into next st, 1sc) around. *18sc*

Rnd 4: (Work 2sc into next st, 2sc) around. *24sc*

M and L sizes only:

Rnd 5: (Work 2sc into next st, 3sc) around. *30sc*

L size only:

Rnd 6: (Work 2sc into next st, 4sc) around. *36sc*

All sizes:

Work even in sc until mittens measure 3½(4:4¼)in (9[10:11]cm) from tip.

THUMB OPENING

Next rnd: Ch 4(5:5), skip next 4(5:5) sc, sc to end of rnd.

Next rnd: Sc into each of next 4(5:5)ch, sc to end of rnd.

Work even on these sts for 5(6:7) further rnds, change to size 7 (4.5mm) hook and work 3(4:5) further rnds.

Fasten off yarn.

Rejoin yarn to any point around thumb opening and work 10(12:12)sc around edge then work even in sc on these sts until thumb measures approx 2in (5cm), or desired length of thumb.

Next rnd: Sc2tog around.

Fasten off yarn and draw in any hole at end of thumb.

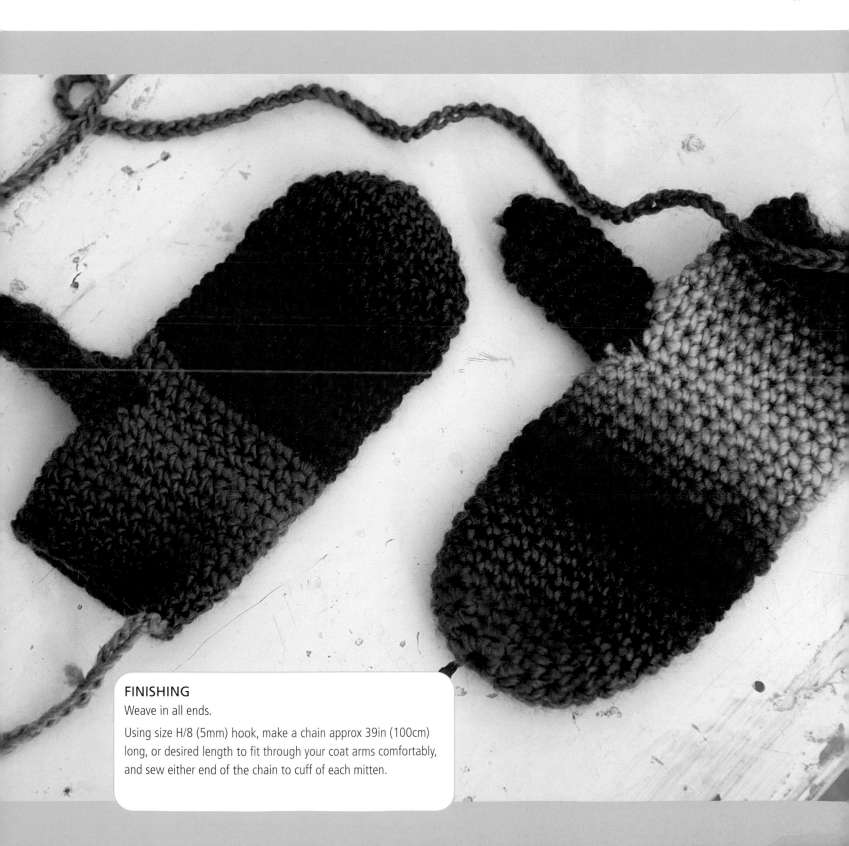

FINISHING

Weave in all ends.

Using size H/8 (5mm) hook, make a chain approx 39in (100cm) long, or desired length to fit through your coat arms comfortably, and sew either end of the chain to cuff of each mitten.

  **Intermediate**

Cowl

A very quick project, worked in the round, so no sewing up! Try using lots of different scraps of yarn for a rainbow-colored neck warmer.

MEASUREMENTS
One size, approx 4in (10cm) wide and 47in (120cm) around.

YARN
1 x 3½oz (100g) ball—approx 144yds (132m)—Artesano Aran, 50% superfine alpaca, 50% Peruvian highland wool, in each of:
Yarn A: shade 2184, meadle
Yarn B: shade 5083, lomond

ALTERNATIVE YARNS
Use any Aran or worsted weight yarn to achieve the same-sized cowl, or try different yarns—the resulting cowl will just come out smaller or larger.

GAUGE (TENSION)
Approx 3 grouped double crochets and 7 rows to 4in (10cm) using size H/8 (5mm) hook or size required to obtain correct gauge.

NOTIONS
*Size H/8 (5mm) crochet hook
*Darning needle

PATTERN NOTES
Cowl is worked in the round, do not turn throughout.

COWL
Using size H/8 (5mm) hook and yarn A, ch 120, join to first ch with a ss, trying not to twist chain.

Rnd 1: Ch 3, 2dc into bottom of same ch, ch 1, skip 2ch, *3dc into next ch, ch 1, skip 2ch; rep from * to end of rnd, join to top of t-ch with a ss.

Rnd 2: Ss to next 1-ch sp, ch 3, 2dc into 1-ch sp, ch 1, *3dc into next 1-ch sp, ch 1; rep from * to end of rnd, join to top of t-ch with a ss.

Fasten off yarn A.

Rnd 3: Join yarn B to any 1-ch sp with a ss, ch 3, 2dc into 1-ch sp, ch 1, *3dc into next 1-ch sp, ch 1; rep from * to end of rnd, join to top of t-ch with a ss.

Fasten off yarn B.

Rnd 4: Join yarn A to any 1-ch sp with a ss, ch 3, 2dc into 1-ch sp, ch 1, *3dc into next 1-ch sp, ch 1; rep from * to end of rnd, join to top of t-ch with a ss.

Fasten off yarn A.

Rnd 5: Rep rnd 3.

Fasten off yarn B.

Rnd 6: Join yarn A to any 1-ch sp with a ss, ch 3, 2dc into 1-ch sp, ch 1, *3dc into next 1-ch sp, ch 1; rep from * to end of rnd, join to top of t-ch with a ss.

Rnd 7: Ss to next 1-ch sp, ch 3, 2dc into 1-ch sp, ch 1, *3dc into next 1-ch sp, ch 1; rep from * to end of rnd, join to top of t-ch with a ss.

Fasten off yarn.

FINISHING
Weave in ends.

Carefully press the cowl into shape on a soft surface. This is known as blocking.

 Intermediate

Flower Earmuffs

If you don't like hats, but can't stand having cold ears, earmuffs are for you—and they are also great for when your friends just talk too loudly!

MEASUREMENTS
One size, approx 11½in (29cm) from center of one earmuff, across strap, to center of other earmuff.

YARN
1 x 1¾oz (50g) ball—approx 131yds (120m)—Rico Essentials Merino DK, 100% merino in each of:
Yarn A: shade 19, mulberry
Yarn B: shade 01, rose
Yarn C: shade 04, acacia

ALTERNATIVE YARNS
Any DK or light worsted weight yarn will do to achieve the same size earmuffs; choose something very warm, soft, and cozy!

GAUGE (TENSION)
Approx 22 sts and 20 rows to 4in (10cm) in sc using size G/6 (4mm) crochet hook or size required to obtain correct gauge.

NOTIONS
∗Size G/6 (4mm) crochet hook
∗Darning needle
∗Toy stuffing

PATTERN NOTES
Earpieces are worked in the round, do not turn throughout. Rounds worked in spirals—do not join rounds. Place a marker in first stitch of round to mark beginning of rounds and count rounds, moving marker up every round.
Flowers are worked in the round, joining each round with a ss.
Strap is worked straight, turn at end of each row.

STRAP
Using size G/6 (4mm) crochet hook and yarn A, ch 13.

Row 1: Work 1sc into 2nd ch from hook, work 1sc into each ch to end of row, turn. *12sc*

Row 2: Ch 1, sc into each st across row, turn.

Rep last row until strap is approx 11in (28cm) long.

Fasten off yarn.

EARPIECES
(make 4)
Using size G/6 (4mm) crochet hook and yarn A, ch 2.

Rnd 1: Work 6sc into first ch made, do not join rnd.

Rnd 2: Work 2sc into each sc around. *12sc*

Rnd 3: (Work 2sc into next st, 1sc) around. *18sc*

Rnd 4: (Work 2sc into next st, 2sc) around. *24sc*

Rnd 5: (Work 2sc into next st, 3sc) around. *30sc*

Rnd 6: (Work 2sc into next st, 4sc) around. *36sc*

Rnd 7: (Work 2sc into next st, 5sc) around. *42sc*

Rnd 8: (Work 2sc into next st, 6sc) around. *48sc*

Rnd 9: (Work 2sc into next st, 7sc) around. *54sc*

Rnd 10: (Work 2sc into next st, 8sc) around. *60sc*

Fasten off yarn.

FLOWERS
Using size G/6 (4mm) crochet hook and yarn A, ch 6 and join into a ring with a ss into first ch.

Rnd 1: Ch 1, work 12sc into ring, join rnd with a ss.

Fasten off yarn A and join in yarn B to any sc.

Rnd 2: 1sc in same st as join (ch 5, skip 1sc, sc into next st) six times, finishing last rep with a ss into next st. *6 petals*

Rnd 3: (Work 9sc into next ch sp, ss into sc) around.

Fasten off yarn B and join yarn A to any sc, work 1 rnd in sc all around petal edges.

Fasten off yarn.

TIES

Using size G/6 (4mm) crochet hook and yarns B and C held together, crochet two lengths of chain, each approx in 20in (50cm) long.

FINISHING

Weave in all ends.

Sew two circles together around edge, leaving a hole to stuff. Fill ear piece with toy stuffing to desired fullness and then sew up rem hole. Rep with rem two circles.

Sew a flower to each earpiece.

Sew an earmuff to either end of the strap, with flowers facing out.

Attach a chain to bottom of each earmuff to tie.

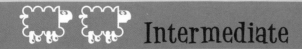 Intermediate

Hat With Earflaps

Keep warm and cozy in this snuggly hat. I've decorated the earflaps with pompoms on strings, but you could leave them plain if you prefer.

MEASUREMENTS
Finished hat approx 22½in (57cm) unstretched.

YARN
1 x 1¾oz (50g) ball—approx 81yds (75m)—Sirdar Click Chunky with wool, 70% acrylic, 30% wool, in each of:
Yarn A: shade 165, blue
Yarn B: shade 142, lamb

ALTERNATIVE YARNS
Any chunky yarn will work well for this project.

GAUGE (TENSION)
Approx 12 sts and 9 rows to 4in (10cm) over hdc using size H/8 (5mm) hook or size required to obtain correct gauge.

NOTIONS
*Size H/8 (5mm) crochet hook
*Darning needle
*Pompom maker

PATTERN NOTES
Hat is worked in the round, do not turn throughout.
Earflaps are worked straight.
Yarn is not fastened off after each color change, and you do not need to join yarn to each new row once it has been joined in. Simply carry the yarn at the back of the work, and pick up and work the new yarn in the next stitch when instructed. Do not pull the yarn too tight when changing color as this will affect the stretch of the hat.

HAT
Using size H/8 (5mm) hook and yarn A, ch 2.

Rnd 1: Work 6hdc into first ch made, join rnd with a ss.

Rnd 2: Work 2hdc into each st around, join rnd with a ss. *12hdc*

Rnd 3: Work 2hdc into each st around, join rnd with a ss. *24hdc*

Rnd 4: (Work 2hdc into next st, 1hdc) around, join rnd with a ss. *36hdc*

Rnd 5: (Work 2hdc into next st, 2hdc) around, join rnd with a ss. *48hdc*

Change to yarn B and work 1 rnd even in sc.

Change back to yarn A.

Rnd 7: (Work 2hdc into next st, 6hdc) around, join rnd with a ss. *54hdc*

Change to yarn B and work 1 rnd even in sc.

Change back to yarn A.

Work 2 rnds even in hdc.

Change to yarn B.

Work 4 rnds even in hdc.

Change to yarn A and work 3 rows even in hdc.

EARFLAP
Work even for earflap as folls:

Row 1: Work 12hdc, turn leaving rem sts unworked.

Row 2: Hdc2tog, hdc to last 2 sts, hdc2tog, turn. *10hdc*

Rep last row until 4 sts rem.

Fasten off yarn.

Rejoin yarn A to 17th st along from last earflap and work as for first earflap.

BORDER

Join yarn B to any point around edge of hat and work a row of sc evenly around entire edge, including earflaps. Do not turn.

Work one further row in sc.

Fasten off yarn

FINISHING

Weave in ends and block lightly.

Make two multi-colored pompoms approx 4in (10cm) diameter using strands of yarn A and B held together.

Work two chains approx 20in (50cm) long and attach one to bottom of each earflap. Attach pompoms to chains.

Chapter 3

Accessories

Easy

Headband

A basic strip of crochet can be easily turned into a headband, with a cute bow to hide the seam and add extra prettiness.

MEASUREMENTS
Headband is approx 2¼in (5.5cm) wide and to fit head approx 17¼(19:20½)in [44(48:52)cm] around, although it is easy to adapt to fit your own head.

YARN
1 x 1¾oz (50g) ball—approx 191yds (175m)—Sirdar Snuggly Kisses DK, 55% nylon, 45% acrylic, in shade 0754, pink

ALTERNATIVE YARNS
Any DK or light worsted weight yarn will work well for this project.

GAUGE (TENSION)
Approx 21 sts and 14 rows to 4in (10cm) over hdc using size D/3 (3.25mm) hook or size required to obtain correct gauge.

NOTIONS
*Size D/3 (3.25mm) crochet hook
*Darning needle

HEADBAND
Using size D/3 (3.25mm) hook, ch 14.

Row 1: Work 1hdc into 2nd ch from hook, then 1hdc into each ch to end of row. *12hdc*

Row 2: Ch 2, work 1hdc into each st to end of row.

Rep last row until headband is approx 17¼(19:20½)in [44(48:52)cm] long, or desired head circumference, allowing for stretch.

Fasten off yarn.

BOW
Using size D/3 (3.25mm) hook, ch 16.

Row 1: Work 1hdc into 2nd ch from hook, then 1hdc into each ch to end of row. *14hdc*

Row 2: Ch 2, work 1hdc into each st to end of row.

Rep last row until strip is approx 4in (10cm) long.

Fasten off yarn.

Using size D/3 (3.25mm) hook, ch 8.

Row 1: Work 1hdc into 2nd ch from hook, then 1hdc into each ch to end of row. *6hdc*

Row 2: Ch 2, work 1hdc into each st to end of row.

Rep last row until strip is approx 4½in (11cm) long.

Fasten off yarn.

FINISHING

Sew ends of headband together to make a loop.

Sew larger bow strip over seam on headband. Wrap small bow strip around the center of larger bow strip and headband, sewing ends together at back of headband to create gathered bow.

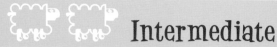 Intermediate

Strand of Beads

Make your strand of beads as long or short as you wish, and with as many differently sized and colored beads threaded on as your heart desires!

MEASUREMENTS

Small beads approx ¾in (2cm) in diameter.
Medium beads approx 1in (2.5cm) in diameter.
Large beads approx 1½in (4cm) in diameter.

YARN

1 x 3½oz (100g) ball—approx 437yds (400m)—DMC Petra no 5, 100% long staple cotton, in each of:
Yarn A: shade 5415, silver
Yarn B: shade 5800, blue
Yarn C: shade 5745, yellow
Yarn D: shade 5149, pink
Yarn E: shade L3821, gold metallic

ALTERNATIVE YARNS

Any fine crochet thread will do for beads of this dimension, although you can use any weight of yarn and scraps from other projects and the beads will just come out different sizes.

GAUGE (TENSION)

Exact gauge isn't essential for this project but make sure that you crochet tightly so that the stuffing does not show.

NOTIONS

∗Size B/1 (2.25mm) crochet hook
∗Stitch marker
∗Darning needle
∗Toy stuffing

PATTERN NOTES

Beads are worked in the round, do not turn throughout. Rounds worked in spirals, do not join into rounds. Place a marker in first stitch of round to mark beginning of rounds and count rounds, moving marker up every round. Begin stuffing ball from last even round to ensure an evenly filled ball.

SMALL BEAD

Using size B/1 (2.25mm) crochet hook and any color, work 2 ch.

Rnd 1: Work 6sc into first ch made, do not join round.

Rnd 2: Work 2sc into each sc around. *12sc*

Work three rnds even in sc without increasing, then begin to stuff bead.

Begin to decrease as follows:

Rnd 6: (Sc2tog) around until you can decrease no more.

Fasten off yarn and sew up final hole to secure.

MEDIUM BEAD

Using size B/1 (2.25mm) crochet hook and any color, work 2 ch.

Rnd 1: Work 6sc into first ch made, do not join round.

Rnd 2: Work 2sc into each sc around. *12sc*

Rnd 3: Work (1sc, 2sc into next st) around. *18sc*

Work five rnds even in sc without increasing, then begin to stuff bead.

Begin to decrease as follows:

Rnd 9: (1sc, sc2tog) around. *12sc*

Rnd 10: (Sc2tog) around until you can decrease no more.

Fasten off yarn and sew up final hole to secure.

LARGE BEAD

Using size B/1 (2.25mm) crochet hook and any color, work 2 ch.

Rnd 1: Work 6sc into first ch made, do not join round.

Rnds 2–3: Work 2sc into each sc around. *24sc*

Work seven rnds even in sc without increasing, then begin to stuff bead.

Begin to decrease as follows:

Rnds 11–12: (Sc2tog) around until you can decrease no more.

Fasten off yarn and sew up final hole to secure.

CHAIN

Using size B/1 (2.25mm) hook and yarn E, work a chain as long as you wish the necklace to be. Fasten off yarn.

FINISHING

Thread chain into large darning needle. Thread beads at random onto chain and fasten ends of chain together to secure.

For bracelet version, make a length of chain that fits around your wrist, plus 1½in (4cm), ss into a ch approx 1½in (4cm) away from hook to create a loop and fasten off yarn. Thread some small beads onto the chain and sew last bead to non-looped end of chain. Fasten bracelet by wrapping round wrist, then inserting final bead through end loop of chain.

 **Easy**

Belt

An extremely simple belt, which can easily be made longer or shorter or wider as you wish.

MEASUREMENTS

One size, 1in (2.5cm) wide and 36in (92cm) long.

YARN

1 x 1¾oz (50g) ball—approx 137yds (125m)—of Debbie Bliss Ecobaby, 100% Organic Cotton, in each of:

Yarn A: shade 04, aqua
Yarn B: shade 14, lemon
Yarn C: shade 23, peach
Yarn D: shade 24, salmon

ALTERNATIVE YARNS

Any 4ply to sportweight yarn will do here, but very small amounts of yarn are used so scraps left over from other projects are perfect. You could also use other weights of yarn and the belt will simply come out longer or shorter.

GAUGE (TENSION)

Approx 20 sts and 13.5 rows to 4in (10cm) in hdc using size D/3 (3.25mm) hook or size required to obtain correct gauge.

NOTIONS

∗Size D/3 (3.25mm) crochet hook
∗Two very small buttons to fit through holes of stitches to fasten belt—approx ½in (1cm) diameter
∗Sewing needle and thread

BELT

Using size D/3 (3.25mm) hook and yarn A, ch 172.

Row 1: Work 1hdc into 2nd ch from hook, work 1 hdc into each ch to end of row, turn. *170sts*

Change to yarn B, fasten off yarn A, and work 1 row even in hdc, turn.

Change to yarn C, fasten off yarn B, and work 1 row even in hdc, turn.

Change to yarn D, fasten off yarn C, and work 1 row even in hdc.

Fasten off yarn.

FINISHING

Weave in ends.

Sew two buttons to one end of belt. To fasten around waist, insert buttons through holes between stitches at desired length.

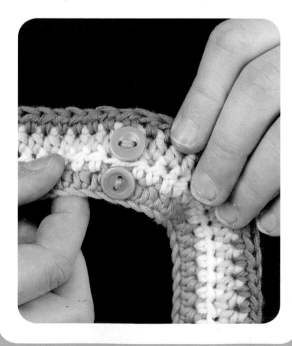

 **Easy**

Flowers

It's so easy to work in the round and create fast and simply stunning brooches or hair clips. Adorn these little lovelies with buttons or beads for added sparkle.

MEASUREMENTS
One size.
Loopy flower approx 2¾in (7cm) diameter.
Small daisy approx 2½in (6cm) diameter.
Large daisy approx 3½in (9cm) diameter.
Small flower approx 1½in (4cm) diameter.

YARN
1 x 1¾oz (50g) ball—approx 131yds (120m)—Rico Essentials Merino DK, 100% merino in each of:
Yarn A: shade 65, yellow
Yarn B: shade 20, lilac
Yarn C: shade 04, acacia
Yarn D: shade 10, magenta
Yarn E: shade 01, rose
Yarn F: shade 45, mint
Yarn G: shade 19, mulberry

ALTERNATIVE YARNS
Use any scraps of yarn in differing weights here—simply change the hook accordingly. The flowers will turn out different sizes, but that will just add to their charm! This project uses very small amounts of yarn, so is perfect for using up leftovers from other projects.

GAUGE (TENSION)
Exact gauge isn't essential for this project.

NOTIONS
*Size E/4 (3.5mm) crochet hook
*Darning needle
*Brooch back, safety pin or hairclip for fastening
*Buttons/beads for embellishment if desired

PATTERN NOTES
Daisies and small flower worked in the round, do not turn throughout. The loopy flower is worked in rows.

DAISIES
First round same for both daisies:
Using size E/4 (3.5mm) hook and yarn A, ch 6 and join into ring with a ss.
Rnd 1: Work 20sc into ring, join rnd with a ss.
Fasten off yarn A.

LARGE DAISY
Join yarn B to any sc with a ss.
Rnd 2: Ch 20, (ss into next sc, ch 20) around, join last petal to bottom of first ch with a ss.
Fasten off yarn and weave in ends.

SMALL DAISY
Join yarn B to any sc with a ss.
Rnd 2: Ch 10, (skip 1 sc, ss into next sc, ch 10) around, join last petal to bottom of first ch with a ss.
Fasten off yarn and weave in ends.

LOOPY FLOWER
Using size E/4 (3.5mm) hook and yarn C, ch 5.
Row 1: Work 1 sc into 2nd ch from hook, 1 sc into each ch to end of row, turn. *4sc*
Row 2: Ch 30, sc in sc at base of ch, sc to end of row, turn.
Row 3: Ch 1, sc to end of row, turn.
Row 4: Ch 30, sc in sc at base of ch, sc to end of row, turn.
Rep rows 3–4 eight times more.
Change to yarn D.
Next row: Ch 1, sc to end of row, turn.
Next row: Ch 25, sc in sc at base of ch, sc to end of row, turn.
Next row: Ch 1, sc to end of row, turn.
Rep last two rows nine times more.
Change to yarn E.
Next row: Ch 1, sc to end of row, turn.
Next row: Ch 20, sc in sc at base of ch, sc to end of row, turn.

Next row: Ch 1, sc to end of row, turn.

Rep last two rows nine times more.

Fasten off.

Roll up strip with smaller loops in the middle and secure in place by sewing together through the sc section at the back.

SMALL FLOWER

Using size E/4 (3.5mm) hook and yarn F, ch 3.

Rnd 1: Work 5sc into first ch, join rnd with a ss.

Rnd 2: Work 2sc into each st around, join rnd with a ss. *10sc*

Rnd 3: (1sc, 2sc into next st) around, join rnd with a ss. *15sc*

Fasten off yarn F.

Join yarn G to any sc with a ss.

Rnd 4: Ch 1, 2dc into each of next 2 sts, (1sc, 2dc into each of next 2 sts) to end of rnd, join rnd with a ss in 1-ch. *5 petals made*

Fasten off yarn and weave in ends.

FINISHING

Attach brooch back, safety pin, or hairclip to the back of each flower to secure. Sew buttons and beads to the fronts for embellishment if desired.

Heart and Star Hairclips

Crochet is the perfect way to cover boring hairclips and slides in your favorite color.
Add a cute heart or star to really make them shine.

MEASUREMENTS
One size, hearts and stars approx
1in (2.5cm) wide.

YARN
1 x 3½oz (100g) ball—approx
306yds (280m)—DMC Petra
no 3, 100% long staple cotton,
in each of:
Yarn A: shade, 5321, red
Yarn B: shade, 53904, ice blue
Yarn C: shade, 53900, green

ALTERNATIVE YARNS
Any no 3 weight crochet cotton will
do here for slides of this dimension,
although you can use any weight of
yarn and the shapes will be different
sizes. These projects only use very
small amounts of yarn, so it is a
perfect way of using up scraps of
yarn left from other projects.

GAUGE (TENSION)
Exact gauge isn't essential for
this project.

NOTIONS
∗Size D/3 (3.25mm) crochet hook
∗Darning needle
∗Hairclips

HAIRCLIP
Using size D/3 (3.25mm) hook and any color, join yarn to any point hair
clip with a ss.

Work sc evenly all round the clip, through the center hole, to cover.

Fasten off yarn.

HEART
Rnd 1: Ch 2, work 9sc into 2nd ch from hook, join rnd with a ss.

Rnd 2: Ch 1, sc into next st, (1hdc, 5dc, 1hdc) all into next st, ss into
next st, (1hdc, 5dc, 1hdc) all into next st, sc to end of end, ss into first
ch to join rnd.

Fasten off yarn.

STAR
Rnd 1: Ch 2, work 10sc into 2nd ch from hook, join rnd with a ss.

Rnd 2: (Ch 2, 1dc into next st, ch 2, ss into next st) five times.

Fasten off yarn.

FINISHING
Sew heart or star to fat end of clip to hide uncovered portion.

Easy

Bracelets

These simple bracelet tubes can be adapted to fit you perfectly. Make lots of them in different colors to go with all your favorite clothes.

MEASUREMENTS
To fit you!

YARN
1 x 1¾oz (50g) ball—approx 104yds (95m) – Sirdar Snuggly Baby Bamboo, 80% bamboo, 20% wool, in each of:
Yarn A: shade 162, toy box red
Yarn B: shade 160, paint box pink
Yarn C: shade 161, baby berries purple
Yarn D: shade 159, jack-in-the-box turquoise

ALTERNATIVE YARNS
Any DK or light worsted weight yarn will make the same sized bracelets. However, you could use long scraps of yarn of any weight to make them, changing your hook size to match, and they will simply come out in different widths.

GAUGE (TENSION)
Exact gauge isn't essential for this project.

NOTIONS
*Size E/4 (3.5mm) crochet hook
*Stitch marker
*Darning needle

PATTERN NOTES
Bracelets are worked in the round, do not turn throughout. Rounds worked in spirals, do not join into rounds. Place a marker in first stitch of round to mark beginning of rounds and count rounds, moving marker up every round.

BRACELET
Using size E/4 (3.5mm) hook and any yarn, ch 8 and join into a ring with a ss into first ch made.

Rnd 1: Ch 1, work 1sc(blo) into each ch around, do not join rnd.

Rnd 2: Work 1sc(blo) into each ch around, do not join rnd.

Rep last rnd until bracelet measures approx 7in (18cm), or length to fit your wrist allowing for stretch over hand.

Fasten off yarn.

FINISHING
Sew two open ends together neatly to form a circle.

 **Easy**

Legwarmers

Crochet these cozy legwarmers in one shade or in candy stripes. They look great with ballet flats or with ankle boots.

MEASUREMENTS
One size, approx 10¼in (26cm) long and 5½in (14cm) wide, but you can make them longer or shorter by working more rounds as desired.

YARN
1 x 1¾oz (50g) ball—approx 109yds (100m)—Rico Essentials Soft Merino Aran, 100% merino wool, in each of:
Yarn A: shade 041, eucalyptus
Yarn B: shade 015, fuchsia
Yarn C: shade 050, pistachio

ALTERNATIVE YARNS
Any Aran or worsted weight yarn will work well for this project.

GAUGE (TENSION)
Approx 11 sts and 10 rows to 4in (10cm) in pattern using size H/8 (5mm) hook or size required to obtain correct gauge.

NOTIONS
∗Size 7 (4.5mm) and size H/8 (5mm) crochet hooks
∗Darning needle

LEGWARMER
(make 2)

Using size 7 (4.5mm) hook and yarn A, ch 34, join into a ring with a ss into first ch.

Rnd 1: Ch 2, skip next ch, (sc into next ch, ch 1, skip next ch) to end, join rnd with a ss.

Rnd 2: Ch 1, sc into 1-ch sp, (ch 1, sc into 1-ch sp) to end, join rnd with a ss.

Rnd 3: Ch 2, (sc into next 1-ch sp, 1 ch) to end, join rnd with a ss.

Change to yarn B and larger hook.

Rnd 4: Ch 3, work 1dc into each sc and 1-ch sp around, join rnd with a ss. *34sts*

Change to yarn C and work two rnds even in dc.

∗∗Change to yarn A and work one rnd even in sc.

Change to yarn B and work one rnd even in dc.

Change to yarn C and work two rnds even in dc.∗∗

Rep from ∗∗ to ∗∗ three times more, or until desired length of legwarmer has been reached.

Change to yarn A and smaller hook.

Next rnd: Ch 2, skip next dc (sc into next dc, ch 1, skip next dc) to end, join rnd with a ss.

Next rnd: Ch 1, sc into 1-ch sp, (ch 1, sc into 1-ch sp) to end, join rnd with a ss.

Next rnd: Ch 2, (sc into next 1-ch sp, ch 1) to end, join rnd with a ss.

Fasten off yarn.

FINISHING
Weave in ends.

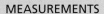 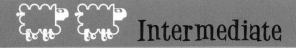 Intermediate

Squares Scarf

Granny squares are traditional, fun, and easy to make, and once you start on them, you will easily become hooked! Join lots of squares together to make a lovely, simple scarf.

MEASUREMENTS
One size, approx 6 x 44in (15 x 112cm).

YARN
1 x 1¾oz (50g) ball—approx 98yds (90m)—of Patons Fairytale Dreamtime DK, 100% pure wool, in each of:
Yarn A: shade 4953, pink
Yarn B: shade 4954, lilac
Yarn C: shade 4957, turquoise
Yarn D: shade 4952, lime
Yarn E: shade 4960, yellow

ALTERNATIVE YARNS
Any DK or light worsted weight yarn will do to achieve the same size scarf, but you can use any yarn you like, the scarf will simply come out a different size!

GAUGE (TENSION)
Each square measures approx 3¼ x 3¼in (8 x 8cm) using a size 7 (4.5mm) hook.

NOTIONS
∗Size 7 (4.5mm) crochet hook
∗Darning needle

SQUARE
(make as many as required, scarf shown has 28)

Using any yarn, and size 7 (4.5mm) hook, ch 4, join to first ch with a ss to form ring.

Rnd 1: Ch 3 (counts as first dc), 2dc in ring, ch 3, (3dc in ring, ch 3) three times, join rnd with a ss to top of first ch, ss to next 3-ch sp.

Rnd 2: Ch 3 (counts as first dc), work (2dc, ch 3, 3dc) all in same 3-ch sp, ch 1, *work (3dc, ch 3, 3dc) all in next 3-ch sp, ch 1; rep from * twice more, join rnd with a ss to top of first ch, ss to next 3-ch sp.

Rnd 3: Ch 3 (counts as first dc), work (2dc, ch 3, 3dc) all in same sp for corner, ch 1, 3dc in next 1-ch sp, ch 1, *work (3dc, ch 3, 3dc) all in next 3-ch sp for corner, ch 1, 3dc in next 1-ch sp, ch 1; rep from * around, join rnd with a ss to top of first ch, ss to next 3-ch sp.

Fasten off yarn.

FINISHING
Using darning needle and matching yarns, sew all squares together with whip stitch to make a scarf two squares wide and 14 squares long.

 Easy

Bird Bag

A sweet and simple book bag, you can easily make yours into any creature that you wish—ours is a robin redbreast. Try stripes for a tiger!

MEASUREMENTS
One size, approx 9½ x 9¾in (24 x 25cm).

YARN
1 x 3½oz (100g) ball—approx 144yds (132m)—Artesano Aran, 50% superfine alpaca, 50% Peruvian highland wool, in each of:
Yarn A: shade 0042, wester
Yarn B: shade c969, ash

ALTERNATIVE YARNS
Use any Aran or worsted weight yarn to achieve the same-sized bag, or try different yarns—the resulting bag will just come out smaller or larger.

GAUGE (TENSION)
Approx 14 hdc and 12 rows to 4in (10cm) in hdc using size H/8 (5mm) hook or size required to obtain correct gauge.

NOTIONS
*Size H/8 (5mm) crochet hook
*Darning needle
*Felt and buttons for features
*Sewing needle and thread

BAG
Using yarn A, ch 72.

Row 1: Work 1 hdc into 3rd ch from hook, 1hdc in each ch to end of row, turn. *70hdc*

Row 2: Ch 2, hdc into each st across row, turn.

Work even in hdc as row 2, until work measures approx 7in (18cm).

Change to yarn B and work a further 2½in (6cm) even in hdc.

Fasten off yarn.

STRAPS
(make 2)

Using yarn A, ch 8.

Row 1: Work 1 hdc into 3rd ch, from hook, 1hdc in each ch to end of row, turn. *6hdc*

Row 2: Ch 2, hdc into each st across row, turn.

Work even in hdc as row 2, until work measures approx 20in (50cm).

Fasten off yarn.

FINISHING
Right side facing, fold fabric in half widthways and backstitch open side and bottom seams together. Turn bag right side out.

Using felt and buttons, sew on the required features to the front of the bag: this robin has felt and button eyes and a felt beak.

Sew a strap to the top inner edge of each side of bag, stitching either end 2½in (6cm) in from either side.

Chapter 4

Bedroom Essentials

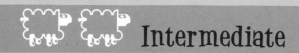 Intermediate

Granny Square Pillow

Once you know how to make granny squares, you can make them as big as you like! Just keep adding rounds as the pattern explains.

MEASUREMENTS
One size, approx 20 x 20in (50 x 50cm).

YARN
1 x 1¾oz (50g) ball—approx 98yds (90m)—Debbie Bliss Cashmerino Aran, 55% merino wool, 33% microfiber, 12% cashmere, in each of:

Yarn A: shade 036, purple
Yarn B: shade 037, violet
Yarn C: shade 42, aubergine
Yarn D: shade 43, pink

ALTERNATIVE YARNS
Any Aran or worsted weight yarn will make the same-sized pillow, but you can use any weight of yarn that you wish, the pillow will simply come out smaller or larger.

GAUGE (TENSION)
Exact gauge isn't essential for this project, but approx 3½ groups of 3dc and 8 rows to 4in (10cm) using a size H/8 (5mm) hook or size required to obtain correct gauge.

NOTIONS
∗Size H/8 (5mm) crochet hook
∗Toy stuffing or pillow form measuring 20 x 20in (50 x 50cm)
∗2 x squares of fabric approx 21¼ x 21¼in (53 x 53cm)
∗Sewing needle and thread

PILLOW

Using size H/8 (5mm) hook and yarn A, ch 4, join to first ch with a ss to form ring.

Rnd 1: Ch 3 (counts as first dc), 2dc in ring, ch 3, (3dc in ring, ch 3) three times, join rnd with a ss to top of first ch, ss to next 3-ch sp.

Rnd 2: Ch 3 (counts as first dc), work (2dc, ch 3, 3dc) all in same 3-ch sp, ch 1, *work (3dc, ch 3, 3dc) all in next 3-ch sp, ch 1; rep from * twice more, join rnd with a ss to top of first ch, ss to next 3-ch sp.

Rnd 3: Ch 3, work (2dc, ch 3, 3dc) all in same sp for corner, ch 1, 3dc in next 1-ch sp, ch 1, *work (3dc, ch 3, 3dc) all in next 3-ch sp for corner, ch 1, 3dc in next 1-ch sp, ch 1; rep from * around, join rnd with a ss to top of first ch.

Break off yarn A.

Rnd 4: Join yarn B to any 3-ch corner sp, ch 3, work (2dc, ch 3, 3dc) in same sp, ch 1, (3dc in next 1-ch sp, ch 1) twice, *work (3dc, ch 3, 3dc) in next corner sp, ch 1, (3dc in next 1-ch sp, ch 1) twice; rep from * around, join rnd with a ss to top of first ch.

Break off yarn B.

Rnd 5: Join yarn A to any 3-ch corner sp, ch 3, work (2dc, ch 3, 3dc) in same sp, ch 1, (3dc in next 1-ch sp, ch 1) three times, *work (3dc, ch 3, 3dc) in next corner sp, ch 1, (3dc in next 1-ch sp, ch 1) three times; rep from * around, join rnd with a ss to top of first ch.

Break off yarn A.

Rnd 6: Join yarn B to any 3-ch corner sp, ch 3, work (2dc, ch 3, 3dc) in same sp, ch 1, (3dc in next 1-ch sp, ch 1) four times, *work (3dc, ch 3, 3dc) in next corner sp, ch 1, (3dc in next 1-ch sp, ch 1) four times; rep from * around, join rnd with a ss to top of first ch, ss to next 3-ch sp.

Rnd 7: Ch 3, work (2dc, ch 3, 3dc) in same sp, ch 1, (3dc in next 1-ch sp, ch 1) to next corner sp, *work (3dc, ch 3, 3dc) in next corner sp, ch 1, (3dc in next 1-ch sp, ch 1) to next corner sp; rep from * around, join rnd with a ss to top of first ch, ss to next 3-ch sp.

Rep rnd 7 once more.

Break off yarn B.

Rnd 9: Join yarn C to any 3-ch corner sp, ch 3, work (2dc, ch 3, 3dc) in same sp, ch 1, (3dc in next 1-ch sp, ch 1) to next corner sp, *work (3dc, ch 3, 3dc) in next corner sp, ch 1, (3dc in next 1-ch sp, ch 1) to next corner sp; rep from * around, join rnd with a ss to top of first ch. Break off yarn C.

Rnd 10: Join yarn B to any 3-ch corner sp, ch 3, work (2dc, ch 3, 3dc) in same sp, ch 1, (3dc in next 1-ch sp, ch 1) to next corner sp, *work (3dc, ch 3, 3dc) in next corner sp, ch 1, (3dc in next 1-ch sp, ch 1) to next corner sp; rep from * around, join rnd with a ss to top of first ch. Break off yarn B.

Join yarn C to any 3-ch corner sp.

Rnd 11: Ch 3, work (2dc, ch 3, 3dc) in same sp, ch 1, (3dc in next 1-ch sp, ch1) to next corner sp, *work (3dc, ch 3, 3dc) in next corner sp, ch 1, (3dc in next 1-ch sp, ch 1) to next corner sp; rep from * around, join rnd with a ss to top of first ch, ss to next 3-ch sp.

Rep rnd 11 twice more, omitting the ss to next 3-ch sp on the last rnd. Break off yarn C.

Rnd 14: Join yarn D to any 3-ch corner sp, ch 3, work (2dc, ch 3, 3dc) in same sp, ch 1, (3dc in next 1-ch sp, ch 1) to next corner sp, *work (3dc, ch 3, 3dc) in next corner sp, ch 1, (3dc in next 1-ch sp, ch 1) to next corner sp; rep from * around, join rnd with a ss to top of first ch. Break off yarn D.

Rnd 15: Join yarn C to any 3-ch corner sp, ch 3, work (2dc, ch 3, 3dc) in same sp, ch 1, (3dc in next 1-ch sp, ch 1) to next corner sp, *work (3dc, ch 3, 3dc) in next corner sp, ch 1, (3dc in next 1-ch sp, ch 1) to next corner sp; rep from * around, join rnd with a ss to top of first ch. Break off yarn C.

Join yarn D to any 3-ch corner sp.

Rnd 16: Ch 3, work (2dc, ch 3, 3dc) in same sp, ch 1, (3dc in next 1-ch sp, ch 1) to next corner sp, *work (3dc, ch 3, 3dc) in next corner sp, ch 1, (3dc in next 1-ch sp, ch 1) to next corner sp; rep from * around, join rnd with a ss to top of first ch, ss to next 3-ch sp.

Rep rnd 16 once more.

(If you wish to make your pillow/granny square bigger, repeat the last row, changing color as you wish until the piece is the desired size.)

Fasten off yarn.

FINISHING

Weave in ends. Block lightly to shape. Sew crochet piece to front of a pillow of the right size, or make a pillow from fabric. Right sides facing, pin two 21¼ x 21¼in (53 x 53cm) squares of fabric together. Taking a ⅝in (1.5cm) seam allowance, sew around all sides, leaving a hole big enough to stuff pillow if using toy stuffing, or leaving one side open if using pillow form. Stuff pillow or insert pillow form and sew up remaining hole neatly. Sew crocheted granny square to front of pillow with small whip stitches of yarn used to crochet final round.

Easy

Sausage Dog Draft Excluder

Keep your bedroom cozy on cold winter evenings by placing this dog by your door to stop drafts coming under it, or fill the dog with PVC beanbag granules and use him as a doorstop.

MEASUREMENTS
One size, approx 27in (68.5cm) long

YARN
1 x 1¾oz (50g) ball—approx 81yds (75m)—Sirdar Click Chunky with wool, 70% acrylic, 30% wool, in each of:
Yarn A: shade 148, bud
Yarn B: shade 163, really red
Yarn B: shade 171, blueberry

ALTERNATIVE YARNS
Any chunky weight yarn will do to achieve the same size dog, although you could use any weight of yarn and the dog will simply come out a different size.

GAUGE (TENSION)
Exact gauge isn't essential for this project but make sure that you crochet tightly so that the stuffing does not show.

NOTIONS
*Size H/8 (5mm) crochet hook
*Toy stuffing
*Buttons and felt for features
*Sewing needle and thread
*Darning needle

DOG
Using size H/8 (5mm) hook and yarn A, ch 2.

Rnd 1: Work 6sc into first ch made, join rnd with a ss.

Rnd 2: Work 2sc into each sc around, join rnd with a ss. *12sc*

Rnd 3: (Work 2sc into next st, 1sc) around, join rnd with a ss. *18sc*

Rnd 4: (Work 2sc into next st, 2sc) around, join rnd with a ss. *24sc*

Rnd 5: (Work 2sc into next st, 3sc) around, join rnd with a ss. *30sc*

Rnd 6: (Work 2sc into next st, 4sc) around, join rnd with a ss. *36sc*

Rnd 7: (Work 2sc into next st, 5sc) around, join rnd with a ss. *42sc*

Rnd 8: (Work 2sc into next st, 6sc) around, join rnd with a ss. *48sc*

Work 4 rows even in sc without increasing.

Change to yarn B and work 2 rows even.

Change to yarn C and work 2 rows even.

Change to yarn A and work 2 rows even.

Cont even on these 48sts until dog is approx 27in (68.5cm) long, striping as established, then if necessary, change back to yarn A.

Stuff body and then begin to decrease as folls:

Rnd 1: (Sc2tog, 6sc) around, join rnd with a ss. *42sc*

Rnd 2: (Sc2tog, 5sc) around, join rnd with a ss. *36sc*

Rnd 3: (Sc2tog, 4sc) around, join rnd with a ss. *30sc*

Rnd 4: (Sc2tog, 3sc) around, join rnd with a ss. *24sc*

Rnd 5: (Sc2tog, 2sc) around, join rnd with a ss. *18sc*

Rnd 6: (Sc2tog, 1sc) around, join rnd with a ss. *12sc*

Rnd 7: (Sc2tog) around, join rnd with a ss. *6sc*

Fasten off yarn and sew up final hole to secure.

FINISHING

Cut out ears, legs, and tail from felt and sew to the body.

Use felt, buttons, and oddments of yarn to make the dog's face.

Advanced

Heart Sachets

Lavender-filled sachets are fabulous for keeping drawers sweet-smelling, or you can place them on a radiator to infuse a whole room. These are perfect gifts for moms on Mother's Day or Valentine's Day.

MEASUREMENTS
One size, approx 7in (18cm) at widest point and 6½in (16.5cm) long.

YARN
1 x 1¾oz (50g) ball—approx 120yds (112m)—of Artesano Soft Merino Superwash DK, 100% merino superwash, in shade 2083, fuchsia

ALTERNATIVE YARNS
Any DK or light worsted weight yarn will do to achieve the same size heart, although you could use any weight of yarn and the sachet will simply come out a different size.

GAUGE (TENSION)
Exact gauge isn't essential for this project but make sure that you crochet tightly so that the lavender does not come out of the heart.

NOTIONS
*Size E/4 (3.5mm) crochet hook
*Darning needle
*Toy stuffing or pvc beanbag beans infused with lavender oils or lavender pot pourri
*Two pieces of fabric approx 7 x 7in (18 x18cm)

PATTERN NOTES
Pieces worked in the round, do not turn throughout.

HEART
(make 2)

Using size E/4 (3.5mm) hook, ch 3.

Rnd 1: 12hdc into first ch made.

Rnd 2: Ch 2 (counts as a hdc), 2hdc, 5dc into next st, (3hdc, 5dc into next st) twice, join rnd with a ss. *25 sts*

Rnd 3: Ch 2 (counts as a hdc), (hdc to center dc of 5dc, 5dc into center dc) three times, hdc to end of rnd, join with a ss to top of first ch.

Rep last rnd twice more.

Rnd 6: Ch 1, *sc to one st before next dc, miss next st, 2 dc into each of next 5dc, miss one st, sc into next st; rep from * once more, sc to center dc of next 5dc, 5dc into center dc, sc to end of rnd.

Rnd 7: Ch 1, *sc to one st before next dc, miss next st, (2 dc into next st, 1 dc into next st) to next sc, miss one st, sc into next st; rep from * once more, sc to center dc of next 5dc, 5dc into center dc, sc to end of rnd.

Rnd 8: Ch 1, *sc to one st before next dc, miss next st, (2 dc into next st, 1 dc into each of next two sts) to next sc, miss one st, sc into next st; rep from * once more, sc to center dc of next 5dc, 5dc into center dc, sc to end of rnd.

Rnd 9: Ch 1, sc to one st before next dc, miss next st, (2 dc into next st, 1 dc into each of next three sts) to next sc, miss one st, ss into next st, miss next st, over next dcs work (2 dc into next st, 1 dc into each of next three sts), to next sc miss one st, sc to center dc of next 5dc, 5dc into center dc, sc to end of rnd.

Fasten off.

FINISHING

Using a heart piece as a template, cut fabric into two heart shapes, slightly larger than the crocheted piece.

With right sides together, sew up fabric heart with a backstitch all around edge, leaving a seam allowance of approx ½in (1cm) all around. Leave a small gap for stuffing. Turn fabric right way out and stuff heart with chosen filling to desired fullness. Sew up rem gap.

Sew together the two crocheted heart pieces, all around edge, leaving gap in seam for stuffing. Fill with the stuffed fabric heart and sew up rem gap.

Advanced

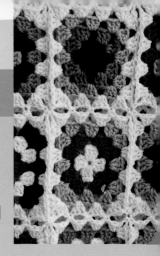

Granny Square Blanket

Granny squares make a stunning and colorful blanket, which is also perfect for using up small scraps of yarn. You can also vary the size to create smaller or larger blankets.

MEASUREMENTS

One size, approx 39 x 39in (100 x 100cm).

YARN

5 x 1¾oz (50g)—approx 490yds (450m)—Debbie Bliss Cashmerino Aran, 55% merino wool, 33% microfiber, 12% cashmere:
Yarn A: shade 101, cream

2 x 1¾oz (50g)—approx 196yds (180m)—Debbie Bliss Cashmerino Aran, 55% merino wool, 33% microfiber, 12% cashmere:
Yarn B: shade 502, green
Yarn C: shade 033, orange
Yarn D: shade 43, light pink
Yarn E: shade 036, purple
Yarn F: shade 205, teal
Yarn G: shade 038, dark pink

ALTERNATIVE YARNS

Any Aran or worsted weight yarns will make the same sized blanket, but you can use any weight of yarn that you wish. This project is perfect for scraps of leftover yarn, and they needn't even be exactly the same weight—so long as they are not too different in size, you can simply use a hook relevant to the heaviest yarn, and hook away!

GAUGE (TENSION)

Not essential, but each square is approx 4¾ x 4¾in (12 x 12cm) using a size H/8 (5mm) hook or size required to obtain correct gauge.

NOTIONS

*Size H/8 (5mm) crochet hook

BASIC SQUARE

(make as many as required, blanket shown has 64)

You can use any color yarn you wish for the first two rounds of each square, but do not use yarn A for the third round.

Using any yarn and size H/8 (5mm) hook, ch 4, join to first ch with a ss to form ring.

Rnd 1: Ch 3 (counts as first dc), 2dc in ring, ch 3, (3dc in ring, ch 3) three times, join rnd with a ss to top of first ch.

Fasten off yarn.

Attach next yarn to any 3-ch corner sp of rnd 1.

Rnd 2: Ch 3 (counts as first dc), work (2dc, ch 3, 3dc) all in same 3-ch sp, ch 1, *work (3dc, ch 3, 3dc) all in next 3-ch sp, ch 1; rep from * twice more, join rnd with a ss to top of first ch.

Fasten off yarn.

Attach next yarn to any 3-ch corner sp of rnd 2.

Rnd 3: Ch 3 (counts as first dc), work (2dc, ch 3, 3dc) all in same sp for corner, ch 1, 3dc in next 1-ch sp, ch 1, *work (3dc, ch 3, 3dc) all in next 3-ch sp for corner, ch 1, 3dc in next 1-ch sp, ch 1; rep from * around, join rnd with a ss to top of first ch.

Fasten off yarn.

Once all central squares have been made, block them all lightly and you can begin to join them with Yarn A.

FIRST SQUARE

Work 4th round complete as folls:

Rnd 4: Using size H/8 (5mm) hook and yarn A, join yarn in any 3-ch corner sp, ch 3, work (2dc, ch 3, 3dc) all in same sp, ch 1, (3dc in next 1-ch sp, ch 1) twice, *work (3dc, ch 3, 3dc) in next 3-ch corner sp, ch 1, (3dc in next 1-ch sp, ch 1) twice; rep from * around, join rnd with a ss to top of first ch.

Now you will have one finished square. However, we are not going to finish each square like this, we are going to join the next square along one side to the first square as we go.

SECOND SQUARE

Work along one side of the square as for first square, then attach to first square as folls:

Rnd 4: Using size H/8 (5mm) hook and yarn A, join yarn in any 3-ch corner sp, ch 3, work (2dc, ch 3, 3dc) all in same sp, ch 1, (3dc in next 1-ch sp, ch 1) twice, ch 1, work 3dc, ch 1 in next 3-ch corner sp, now ss into 2nd ch of any 3-ch corner ch of first square, with RSF, ch 1. Finish off second square corner with final 3dc in 3-ch corner sp of working square.

Now (ss into next 1-ch sp of first square, 3dc in next 1-ch sp of rnd 3 of the second square) twice, ss into next 1-ch sp of first square, 3dc in next 3-ch corner sp of rnd 3 of the second square, ch 1, ss into 2nd ch of next 3-ch of next corner ch of first square, ch 1.

Finish off second square corner with final 3dc in 3-ch corner sp of working square. Now finish off second square edging as a normal granny rnd; (ch 1, 3dc in next 1-ch sp) twice, ch 1, work 3dc, ch 3 and 3dc in next corner sp, (ch 1, 3dc in next 1-ch sp) twice, end ch 1, join rnd with sl st to top of first ch. Fasten off yarn.

Two squares joined.

Join next square to bottom of last square as you joined the first two squares, and continue in the same way until you have a strip of eight squares.

Join first square of next row to right side of top square as previous squares.

Second square of second row, work along one side of the square as usual, then attach to bottom side of first (top) square and right side of square from first row as folls:

Ss into 2nd ch of 3-ch corner ch of bottom right corner of square above, with RSF, ch 1. Finish off working square corner with final 3dc in 3-ch corner sp. Now (ss into next 1-ch sp of first square, 3dc in next 1-ch sp of working square) twice, ss into next 1-ch sp of first square, 3dc in next ch-3 corner sp of working square, ch 1, ss into 2nd ch of next corner ch of first square, ch 1. Finish off working square corner with final 3dc in corner sp.

Now attach working square of first strip by slip stitching into ch sps along joining sides while finishing last rnd of working square as before, then finish final edge, (ch 1, 3dc in next 1-ch sp) twice, end ch 1, join rnd with a ss to top of first ch. Fasten off yarn.

Continue to join squares in this way, along two sides, until eight squares have been joined in one long strip that is two squares wide.

Continue in this way until eight rows of strips eight squares long have been joined together.

FINISHING

Weave in all ends and block lightly to shape.

Intermediate

Zigzag Bolster

A crazily striped bolster for your bed. Have fun mixing and matching all your favorite colors.

MEASUREMENTS

Approx 14in (36cm) wide

YARN

1 x 1¾oz (50g) ball—approx 104yds (95m)—Sirdar Snuggly Baby Bamboo, 80% bamboo, 20% wool, in each of:

Yarn A: shade 144, tom thumb green
Yarn B: shade 157, yellow submarine
Yarn C: shade 149, scooter blue
Yarn D: shade 159, jack-in-the-box turquoise
Yarn E: shade 161, baby berries purple
Yarn F: shade 160, paint box pink
Yarn G: shade 162, toy box red
Yarn H: shade 126, rocking horse red
Yarn I: shade 134, babe pink

ALTERNATIVE YARNS

Any DK or light worsted weight yarn will make the same-sized pillow. However, you could use long scraps of yarn of any weight, changing hook size to match, and the bolster will simply be different dimensions.

GAUGE (TENSION)

15 sts and 15 rows to 4in (10cm) in zigzag patt using size G/6 (4mm) hook or size required to obtain correct gauge.

NOTIONS

∗Size G/6 (4mm) crochet hook
∗Darning needle
∗Toy stuffing, or bolster pad measuring
   15½in (39cm) long and 19½in (49cm) in circumference
∗Two circles of fabric approx 6in (15cm) in diameter

BOLSTER

With size G/6 (4mm) hook and yarn A, ch 98.

Row 1: Work 2sc into 2nd ch from hook, *sc into each of next 7ch, skip 1ch, sc into each of next 7ch, 3sc into next ch; rep from * to end, but work 2sc into last ch instead of 3sc.

Row 2: Ch 1, 2sc into first st, *7sc, skip next 2sc, 7sc, 3sc into next stitch; rep from * to end, but work 2sc into last st instead of 3sc.

Rep row 2 for pattern, changing color after every four rows, until work measures approx 19in (48cm) long.

FINISHING

Sew piece together along the two long edges, fitting the peaks and troughs of the zigzag into each other.

Sew a circle of fabric to one end of the bolster, then fill bolster with toy stuffing or a pad of correct measurements. Sew remaining circle of fabric to open end of bolster.

Intermediate

Bootie Slippers

Simple slippers—which are easily adaptable for your size of foot—are brilliant for keeping your toes cozy while you watch tv, chat online, or do your homework.

MEASUREMENTS
Adjustable to fit your own foot size.

YARN
1 x 1¾oz (50g) ball—approx 109yds (100m)—Rico Essentials Soft Merino Aran, 100% merino wool, in each of:

Yarn A: shade 020, light gray
Yarn B: shade 041, eucalyptus
Yarn C: shade 036, royal blue
Yarn D: shade 050, pistachio
Yarn E: shade 037, navy

ALTERNATIVE YARNS
Any Aran or worsted weight yarn will work well for this project.

GAUGE (TENSION)
17sc and 16 rows to 4in (10cm) over sc using size H/8 (5mm) hook or size required to obtain correct gauge.

NOTIONS
*Size H/8 (5mm) and size C/2 (2.5mm) crochet hooks
*Thick wool felt
*Darning needle

SOLE
Draw around your foot onto a piece of paper to get the basic shape and size of the sole—if one foot is larger than the other, draw around the larger one. Round off the shape so that it flows smoothly, and make it symmetrical so that either slipper fits either foot. Cut two shapes from felt.

Punch holes all round the edge of the felt using a sharp needle or the end of your small crochet hook. Space the holes ¼in (0.5cm) apart and ¼in (0.5cm) in from the outside edge.

SLIPPER
Using the size C/2 (2.5mm) hook and yarn A, work 1sc into each of these holes evenly around the edge of the felt.

Join round with a ss to first sc.

Change to size H/8 (5mm) hook.

Work 5 further rounds of sc evenly on these sts in yarn A.

Rnd 7: Work in sc, decreasing 5 sts evenly over toe sts.

Change to yarn B and work one row even in sc without decreasing.

Change to yarn C.

Rnd 9: Work in sc, decreasing 5 sts evenly over toe sts.

Change to yarn D and work one row even in sc without decreasing.

Change to yarn E.

Rnd 11: Work in sc, decreasing 5 sts evenly over toe sts.

Fasten off yarn.

FINISHING
Sew up seam from toe for 2in (5cm).

Easy

Storage Jars

Make these covers for jars, vases, and tins to store pens, pencils, crochet hooks—or fill them with water to display flowers with colorful style.

MEASUREMENTS

To fit tubular storage containers of approx 2in, 2¾in, and 3½in (5cm, 7cm, and 9cm) in diameter, and of any height.

YARN

1 x 1¾oz (50g) ball—approx 120yds (112m)—of Artesano Soft Merino Superwash DK, 100% merino superwash, in each of:

Yarn A: shade 1291, sea blue
Yarn B: shade 5167, teal
Yarn C: shade 2083, fuchsia
Yarn D: shade 6315, lime green
Yarn E: shade SFN10, cream
Yarn F: shade 7254, sand yellow

ALTERNATIVE YARNS

Any DK or light worsted weight yarn will do here, oddments and leftovers from other projects are perfect for the odd stripes.

GAUGE (TENSION)

Approx 18 sts and 26 rows to 4in (10cm) in sc using size E/4 (3.5mm) hook or size required to obtain correct gauge.

NOTIONS

*Size E/4 (3.5mm) crochet hook
*Darning needle
*Assorted jars and containers

PATTERN NOTES

Pieces are worked in the round, do not turn throughout.

COVER

Begin all jars from rnd 1. For 2in (5cm) jar, work to rnd 5 and then work from the all sizes instruction; for 2¾in (7cm) jar, work to rnd 7 and then work from all sizes instruction; and for 3½in (9 cm) jar, work all rows before completing from all sizes instruction.

Begin with yarn A and then work 1 or 2 row stripes alternately of all colors.

Using size E/4 (3.5mm) hook and yarn A, ch 2.

Rnd 1: Work 6sc into first ch, join into round with a ss.

Rnd 2: Work 2sc into each st around join rnd with a ss. *12sc*

Rnd 3: (1sc, work 2sc into next st) around. *18sc*

Rnd 4: (2sc, work 2sc into next st) around. *24sc*

Rnd 5: (3sc, work 2sc into next st) around. *30sc*

Rnd 6: (4sc, work 2sc into next st) around. *36sc*

Rnd 7: (5sc, work 2sc into next st) around. *42sc*

Rnd 8: (6sc, work 2sc into next st) around, join rnd with a ss. *48sc*

Rnd 8: (7sc, work 2sc into next st) around, join rnd with a ss. *54sc*

Rnd 8: (8sc, work 2sc into next st) around, join rnd with a ss. *60sc*

ALL SIZES:

Work 1 rnd even in sc(blo), join rnd with a ss.

Continue even in sc on these sts until desired height of jar is reached, striping as you wish.

Fasten off yarn.

FINISHING

Weave in ends.

Slip these crocheted "cozies" over a jar or vase and fill with stationery or flowers of your choice.

Playtime

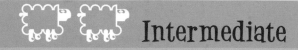 **Intermediate**

Cakes

These little cakes look so sweet you'll find it hard to believe you can't eat them.

MEASUREMENTS
Cupcake approx 4in (10cm) diameter.
Donut approx 4¾in (12cm) diameter.
Sponge cake approx 2½in (6cm) diameter and 3½in (9cm) tall.

YARN
1 x 1¾oz (50g) ball—approx 137yds (125m)—Millamia Merino, 100% merino, in each of:
Yarn A: shade 160, fawn
Yarn B: shade 122, petal
Yarn C: shade 104, claret
Yarn D: shade 124, snow

ALTERNATIVE YARNS
Any DK or light worsted weight yarn will do here but as gauge is not essential, you could try any yarn and the cakes will just come out different sizes. You could also try some metallic yarns for sparkle, or stripe up the colors for different patterns.

GAUGE (TENSION)
Exact gauge isn't essential for this project but make sure that you crochet tightly so that the stuffing does not show.

NOTIONS
∗Size D/3 (3.25mm) crochet hook
∗Darning needle
∗Sewing needle and thread
∗Beads and buttons for decoration
∗Toy stuffing

PATTERN NOTES
Pieces are worked in the round, do not turn throughout. Rounds worked in spirals—do not join rounds unless otherwise stated. Place a marker in first stitch of round to mark beginning of rounds and count rounds, moving marker up every round.

CUPCAKE
Using size D/3 (3.25mm) hook and yarn A, ch 2.

Rnd 1: Work 6sc into first ch, join into round with a ss.

Rnd 2: Work 2sc into each st around join rnd with a ss. *12sc*

Rnd 3: (1sc, work 2sc into next st) around. *18sc*

Rnd 4: (2sc, work 2sc into next st) around. *24sc*

Rnd 5: (3sc, work 2sc into next st) around. *30sc*

Rnd 6: (4sc, work 2sc into next st) around. *36sc*

Rnd 7: (5sc, work 2sc into next st) around. *42sc*

Rnd 8: (6sc, work 2sc into next st) around, join rnd with a ss. *48sc*

Work 1 rnd even in sc(blo), join rnd with a ss.

Work even in sc for seven more rnds, in spirals, do not join rnds.

Next rnd: *Ch 3, ss(tfl) of next st; rep from * all round, join rnd with a ss.

Fasten off yarn A.

Join yarn B to the unworked back loop in any st of last sc rnd.

Next row: Work sc(blo) into each unworked back loop of last sc rnd, join rnd with a ss.

Work four rnds even in sc in spirals, do not join rounds.

Next row: (6sc, sc2tog) around, join rnd with a ss. *42sc*

Work one rnd even without shaping.

Next row: (5sc, sc2tog) around, join rnd with a ss. *36sc*

Work one rnd even without shaping.

Next row: (4sc, sc2tog) around, join rnd with a ss. *30sc*

Work one rnd even without shaping.

Begin to stuff cake to shape, filling until desired fullness.

Next row: (3sc, sc2tog) around, join rnd with a ss. *24sc*

Next row: (2sc, sc2tog) around, join rnd with a ss. *18sc*

Next row: (1sc, sc2tog) around, join rnd with a ss. *12sc*

Next row: (Sc2tog) around, join rnd with a ss. *6sc*

Sew round rem hole and pull up to secure.

FINISHING

Decorate with small round beads for sprinkles and add a large red button or glass bead on top for a cherry if desired.

SPONGE CAKE

Using size D/3 (3.25mm) hook and yarn B, ch 2.

Rnd 1: Work 6sc into first ch.

Rnd 2: Work 2sc into each st around join rnd with a ss. *12sc*

Rnd 3: (1sc, work 2sc into next st) around. *18sc*

Rnd 4: (2sc, work 2sc into next st) around. *24sc*

Rnd 5: (3sc, work 2sc into next st) around. *30sc*

Rnd 6: (4sc, work 2sc into next st) around. *36sc*

Rnd 7: (5sc, work 2sc into next st) around. *42sc*

Rnd 8: (6sc, work 2sc into next st) around. *48sc*

Work 1 rnd even in sc(blo).

Work even in sc(blo) for seven more rnds.

Change to yarn D and work even in sc(blo) for two more rnds.

Change to yarn C and work one rnd even in sc.

Change to yarn D and work even in sc(blo) for two more rnds.

Change to yarn B and work even in sc(blo) for five more rnds.

Next rnd: *6sc(blo), sc2tog(blo); rep from * around. *42sc*

Begin to stuff cake to desired fullness.

Next rnd: (5sc, sc2tog) around. *36sc*

Next rnd: (4sc, sc2tog) around. *30sc*

Next rnd: (3sc, sc2tog) around. *24sc*

Next rnd: (2sc, sc2tog) around. *18sc*

Next rnd: (1sc, sc2tog) around. *12sc*

Next rnd: (Sc2tog) around. *6sc*

Sew round rem hole and pull up to secure.

FINISHING

Sew sprinkles on top of cake with contrast yarn or thread or use bugle beads, if decoration is desired.

DONUT

Using size D/3 (3.25mm) hook and yarn A, ch 65, join into ring with a ss into first ch, being careful not to twist the chain.

Rnd 1: Ch 1, sc into each ch to end of rnd, join to first ch with a ss.

Rnd 2: Ch 1, sc(blo) to end of rnd, join to first ch with a ss.

Work last rnd five times more.

Change to yarn C.

Next rnd: Ch 1, sc into each st to end of rnd, join to first ch with a ss.

Work last round nine times more.

Fasten off.

FINISHING

Sew top edge to bottom edge, without twisting, to form donut, leaving a space for stuffing. Stuff donut to desired fullness, then sew up rem seam.

Decorate with colorful bugle beads or sew on contrasting yarn dashes for sprinkles if desired.

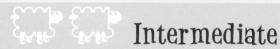

Intermediate

Candy

Fun-to-make pieces of candy that use metallic and bright yarns to represent the colorful and shiny wrappers.

MEASUREMENTS
One size, each piece of candy is approx 4in (10cm) long.

YARN
Yarn A
1 x 3½oz (100g) ball—approx 306yds (280m)—DMC Petra no 3, 100% long staple cotton, in each of:
Shade 5742, yellow
Shade 53845, blue
Shade 5907, green
Shade 53805, pink

Yarn B
1 x ¾oz (20g) ball—approx 164yds (150m)—DMC Metallic Crochet Thread, 60% viscose, 40% metalized polyester, in each of:
Shade L677, gold
Shade L796, blue

ALTERNATIVE YARNS
Any number 5 weight crochet cotton will make candy of this dimension, although you can use any weight of yarn and the candy will just come out different sizes.

GAUGE (TENSION)
Exact gauge isn't essential for this project but make sure that you crochet tightly so that the stuffing does not show.

NOTIONS
∗Size D/3 (3.25mm) crochet hook
∗Darning needle
∗Toy stuffing

PATTERN NOTES
Candy is worked in the round, do not turn throughout. Rounds worked in spirals—do not join rounds. Place a marker in first stitch of round to mark beginning of rounds and count rounds, moving marker up every round.

CANDY
Using size D/3 (3.25mm) hook and any yarn A, ch 20, join into a ring with a ss to first ch.

Rnd 1: Ch 1, sc into each st to end of rnd.

Rnd 2: Sc into each st around.

Rep last row until candy measures approx 3in (8cm) long.

Fasten off yarn.

Join any yarn B to one open edge of candy.

Next rnd: Ch 1, skip 1 sc, 5dc into next st, *skip 1 sc, sc into next st, skip 1 sc, 5dc into next st, rep from * to last st, skip last sc, ss into first ch to join rnd.

Rep last round at opposite end of candy.

FINISHING
Weave in all ends.

Thread a piece of yarn in and out of the stitches all round one end of candy, approx 1in (2.5cm) in from end, pull up thread tightly to draw in end of candy and fasten off securely.

Stuff candy to desired fullness, then sew round opposite end of candy in same way as first end, approx 1in (2.5cm) in from end.

Pirate's Parrot and Eye Patch

A fun dressing-up outfit; attach the parrot to your shoulder and go in search of some gold!

MEASUREMENTS

One size; parrot approx 4¾in (12cm) high.
Eyepatch approx 3in (8cm) at widest point.

YARN

1 x 1¾oz (50g)—136yds (125m)—Anchor Style Creativa Fino, 100% cotton, in each of:
Yarn A: shade 01330, apple green
Yarn B: shade 01320, pink
Yarn C: shade 00108, lilac

ALTERNATIVE YARNS

Any 4ply or sportweight yarn or crochet cotton will work well for this project.

GAUGE (TENSION)

Exact gauge isn't essential for this project but make sure that you crochet tightly so that the stuffing does not show.

NOTIONS

* Size D/3 (3.25mm) crochet hook
* Stitch marker
* Toy stuffing
* Two buttons for eyes
* Fabric to line eye patch
* Darning needle
* Sewing needle and thread
* Large safety pin for pinning parrot to shirt

PATTERN NOTES

Parrot is worked in the round, do not turn throughout. Rounds worked in spirals—do not join rounds. Place a marker in first stitch of round to mark beginning of rounds and count rounds, moving marker up every round. Begin from top of head.
Eye patch worked in the round, join rounds with slip stitches.

PARROT HEAD AND BODY

Using size D/3 (3.25mm) crochet hook and yarn A, ch 2.

Rnd 1: Work 6sc into first ch made, do not join rnd.

Rnd 2: Work 2sc into each sc around. *12sc*

Rnd 3: (Work 2sc into next st, 1sc) around. *18sc*

Rnd 4: (Work 2sc into next st, 2sc) around. *24sc*

Rnd 5: (Work 2sc into next st, 3sc) around. *30sc*

Rnd 6: (Work 2sc into next st, 4sc) around. *36sc*

Rnd 7: (Work 2sc into next st, 5sc) around. *42sc*

Rnd 8: (Work 2sc into next st, 6sc) around. *48sc*

Work 2 rnds even in sc.

Rnd 11: (Work 2sc into next st, 7sc) around. *54sc*

Work 4 rnds even in sc.

Begin to decrease as follows:

Rnd 16: (Sc2tog, 7sc) around. *48sc*

Work 2 rnds even in sc.

Rnd 19: (Sc2tog, 6sc) around. *42sc*

Work 3 rnds even in sc.

Rnd 23: (Sc2tog, 5sc) around. *36sc*

Work 3 rnds even in sc.

Rnd 27: (Sc2tog, 4sc) around,. *30sc*

Work 1 rnd even in sc.

Change to yarn B and work 2 rnds even in sc.

Begin to stuff from now.

Rnd 31: (Sc2tog, 3sc) around. *24sc*

Work three rnds even in sc.

Rnd 35: (Sc2tog, 2sc) around. *18sc*

Work three rnds even in sc.

Rnd 39: (Sc2tog, 1sc) around, join rnd with a ss. *12sc*

Add more stuffing as necessary.

Rnd 40: (Sc2tog) around, join rnd with a ss. *6sc*

Fasten off yarn.

HEAD FEATHERS

Using size D/3 (3.25mm) crochet hook and yarn A, ch 14.

Row 1: Work 1sc into 2nd ch from hook, 1 sc into each ch to end of row. *13sts*

Row 2: Ch 1, (skip next st, (3tr, ch 1, 3tr) into next st, skip next st, 1sc into next st) 3 times.

Fasten off yarn.

BEAK

Using size D/3 (3.25mm) crochet hook and yarn C, ch 12 and join into a ring with a ss to first ch.

Row 1: Ch 1, 1sc into each ch around, join round with a ss.

Rep last row 4 more times.

Next rnd: (Sc2tog) around, join rnd with a ss. *6sc*

Fasten off yarn leaving long tail.

WING

(make 2)

Using size D/3 (3.25mm) hook and yarn C, ch 2.

Rnd 1: Work 6sc into first ch made, do not join rnd.

Rnd 2: Work 2sc into each sc around. *12sc*

Rnd 3: (Work 2sc into next st, 1sc) around. *18sc*

Rnd 4: (Work 2sc into next st, 2sc) to last 3 sts, 3dc into next st, 2sc. *25sts*

Rnd 5: (Work 2sc into next st, 3sc) to 3dc of previous row, sc into first dc, 3dc into next st, sc into each st to end of row. *32sts*

Fasten off yarn.

TAIL FEATHERS

Using size D/3 (3.25mm) crochet hook and yarn C, ch 7.

Row 1: Sc into 2nd ch from hook, sc into each ch to end. *6sc*

Row 2: Ch 1, sc into each st to end of row.

Rep last row 4 times more, then increase 1 st at both ends of next 3 rows. *12sc*

Next row: Ch 1, *skip next st, 3dc into next st, skip next st, sc into next st; rep from * to end of row.

Next row: Ch 1, 3dc into sc, *dc into center dc of next 3dc, 3dc into sc; rep from * to end of row.

Next row: Ch 1, dc into center dc of next 3dc, *3dc into sc, dc into center dc of next 3dc; rep from * across row.

Fasten off yarn.

FINISHING

Sew head feathers to top of parrot's head and tail feathers to tail end of body. Sew a wing to each side of body. Use tail of yarn to sew beak to parrot's face.

EYE PATCH

Using size D/3 (3.25mm) crochet hook and yarn A, ch 6 and join into a ring with a ss to first ch.

Rnd 1: Ch 3, (2tr, ch 3) into ring, (3tr, ch 3) into ring twice more, join rnd with a ss to top of first ch.

Rnd 2: Ss to next 3-ch sp, (ch 3, 2tr, ch 3, 3tr) all into 3-ch sp, *ch 1, (3tr, ch 1, 3tr) all into next 3-ch sp; rep from * once more, ch 1, join rnd with a ss to top of first ch.

Rnd 3: Ss to next 3-ch sp, (ch 3, 2tr, ch 3, 3tr) all into 3-ch sp, *ch 1, 3tr into next 1-ch sp, ch 1, (3tr, ch 1, 3tr) all into next 3-ch sp; rep from * once more, ch 1, 3tr into next 1-ch sp, ch 1, join rnd with a ss to top of first ch.

Fasten off yarn.

FINISHING

Attach yarn to top corner of eye patch and ch approx 20in (50cm) or desired length to comfortably tie round head. Fasten off yarn. Rep with other top corner of eye patch.

Stitch fabric to the reverse of patch to cover holes within the crochet.

 **Intermediate**

Rag Doll

A basic floppy rag doll that you can adapt and embellish to make your own unique character—make outfits for her, change her hair, or give her a different expression.

MEASUREMENTS
One size, approx 12in (30cm) tall.

YARN
1 x 1¾oz (50g) ball—approx 142yds (130m)—of Sirdar Simply Recycled DK, 51% recycled cotton, 40% acrylic, in each of:
Yarn A: shade 11, canvas
Yarn B: shade 16, denim wash
Yarn C: shade 13, clay

ALTERNATIVE YARNS
Any DK or light worsted weight yarn will achieve the same size doll, although you could use any weight of yarn and the toy will simply come out a different size.

GAUGE (TENSION)
Exact gauge isn't essential for this project but make sure that you crochet tightly so that the stuffing does not show.

NOTIONS
∗Size E/4 (3.5mm) crochet hook
∗Stitch marker
∗Toy stuffing
∗Two buttons for eyes
∗Fabric for dress
∗Darning needle
∗Sewing needle and thread

PATTERN NOTES
Pieces are worked in the round, do not turn throughout. Rounds worked in spirals (apart from legs), do not join rounds. Place a marker in first stitch of round to mark beginning of rounds and count rounds, moving marker up every round.

BODY AND HEAD

Using size E/4 (3.5mm) hook and yarn A, ch 2.
Rnd 1: Work 6sc into first ch made, do not join rnd.
Rnd 2: Work 2sc into each sc around. *12sc*
Rnd 3: (Work 2sc into next st, 1sc) around. *18sc*
Rnd 4: (Work 2sc into next st, 2sc) around. *24sc*
Rnd 5: (Work 2sc into next st, 3sc) around. *30sc*
Rnd 6: (Work 2sc into next st, 4sc) around. *36sc*
Rnd 7: (Work 2sc into next st, 5sc) around. *42sc*
Rnd 8: (Work 2sc into next st, 6sc) around. *48sc*
Work one rnd even in sc without increasing.
Rnd 10: (Work 2sc into next st, 7sc) around. *54sc*
Work eight rnds even in sc without increasing.
Begin to decrease as follows:
Rnd 19: (Sc2tog, 7sc) around. *48sc*
Work one rnd even in sc without decreasing.
Rnd 21: (Sc2tog, 6sc) around. *42sc*
Rnd 22: (Sc2tog, 5sc) around. *36sc*
Rnd 23: (Sc2tog, 4sc) around. *30sc*
Stuff head fully.
Work even in sc in spirals on these 30sts until body is approx 3½in (9cm) long.
Stuff body as necessary, ensuring head does not flop.
Next rnd: (Sc2tog, 3sc) around. *24sc*
Next rnd: (Sc2tog, 2sc) around. *18sc*
Next rnd: (Sc2tog, 1sc) around. *12sc*
Next rnd: (Sc2tog) around. *6sc*
Fasten off yarn and sew up final hole to secure.

ARMS
(make 2)
Using size E/4 (3.5mm) hook and yarn A, ch 2.
Rnd 1: Work 5sc into first ch made, do not join rnd.
Rnd 2: Work 2sc into each sc around. *10sc*
Rnd 3: (Work 2sc into next st, 1sc) around. *15sc*
Work even in sc in spirals on these 15sts until arm is approx 3in (8cm) long.

Stuff arm to desired fullness.

Next rnd: (Sc2tog, 1sc) around. *10sc*

Next rnd: (Sc2tog) around. *5sc*

Sew up rem hole.

LEGS

(make 2)

Work in rnds, joining each round with a ss.

Using size E/4 (3.5mm) hook and yarn B, ch 2.

Rnd 1: Work 5sc into first ch made, join rnd with a ss.

Rnd 2: Work 2sc into each sc around, join rnd with a ss. *10sc*

Rnd 3: Work 2sc into each sc around, join rnd with a ss. *20sc*

Work even in sc, joining each round, on these 20sts for a further 6 rnds without increasing.

Change to yarn B and work 3 rnds even.

Change to yarn A and work 3 rnds even.

Cont even on these stitches for a further 4¾in (12cm), in 3-rnd stripes alternately of yarn A and B.

Fasten off yarn.

Stuff legs and sew up tops.

FINISHING

Sew one arm to either side of body, just underneath neck. Sew legs to bottom of body. Embroider face onto doll.

HAIR

Cut 18 lengths of yarn C approximately 20in (50cm) long. Holding lengths together, tie a knot ¾in (2cm) on either side of center of lengths. Plait both ends of yarn beyond knots and secure with small strips of same fabric as dress, tied into a bow. Stitch center of hair to top of head.

DRESS

Cut out two rectangles of fabric approximately 4½in (11cm) long and slightly wider than the body of the doll. Hem bottom and top, then sew one side seam. Wrap dress around doll's body, under arms, and sew up side seam. Sew to body to secure.

 **Easy**

Princess Tiara

A simple-to-make tiara fit for any little princess. I've sewn on pearls, but you can use beads or sew-on jewels if you prefer.

MEASUREMENTS
Purchase headband to fit wearer's head; crocheted section is approx ¾in (2cm) high.

YARN
1 x ¾oz (20g) ball—approx 164yds (150m)—DMC Metallic Crochet Thread, 60% viscose, 40% metalized polyester, in shade L168, silver

ALTERNATIVE YARNS
Any similar weight metallic crochet thread will work well for this project.

GAUGE (TENSION)
Exact gauge isn't essential for this project.

NOTIONS
*Size C/2 (2.75mm) crochet hook
*Darning needle
*Headband
*Beads for embellishment
*Beading needle and thread

TIARA
Using size C/2 (2.75mm) hook, attach yarn to headband and work 42sc around the center section of the headband, turn.

Next row: Sc, (ch 5, skip 3sts, sc into next st) five times, ch 6, skip 4sts, sc into next st, ch 7, skip 5sts, sc into next st, ch 6, skip 4sts, sc into next st, (ch 5, skip 3sts, sc into next st) five times, turn.

Next row: (Work 7sc into next 5-ch sp, ss into sc) five times, 9sc into next ch sp, ss into sc, 11sc into next ch sp, ss into sc, 9sc into next ch sp, ss into sc (work 7sc into next 5-ch sp, ss into sc) five times.

Fasten off yarn.

FINISHING
Sew on beads as desired.

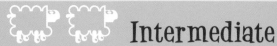

Intermediate

Juggling Balls

Crocheted balls are fabulous for playing games such as Piggy in the Middle or Hacky Sack, and are perfect for learning to juggle. You can stuff these with toy stuffing or for more weight when juggling, fill with beans or PVC beanbag granules.

MEASUREMENTS

One size, approx 2½in (6cm) in diameter.

YARN

1 x 3½oz (100g) ball—approx 437yds (400m)—DMC Petra no 5, 100% long staple cotton, in each of:

Yarn A: shade 5742, yellow
Yarn B: shade 54230, blue
Yarn C: shade 5907, green

ALTERNATIVE YARNS

Any no 5 weight crochet cotton will do here for balls of this dimension, although you can use any weight of yarn and the balls will just come out different sizes.

GAUGE (TENSION)

Exact gauge isn't essential for this project, but ensure that you crochet tightly so that the stuffing does not come through the stitches.

NOTIONS

*Size B/1 (2.25mm) crochet hook
*Darning needle
*Toy stuffing or PVC beanbag beans

PATTERN NOTES

Balls are worked entirely in the round, do not turn work. Begin stuffing ball from rnd 24 to ensure an evenly filled ball. Work 2 rows of each color alternately, or in any order you desire.

BALL

Using size B/1 (2.25mm) crochet hook and any color, ch 2.

Rnd 1: Work 6sc into first ch made, ss to join rnd.

Rnd 2: Ch 1, work 2sc into each sc around, ss to join rnd. *12sc*

Rnd 3: Ch 1, (work 2sc into next st, 1sc) around, ss to join rnd. *18sc*

Rnd 4: Ch 1, (work 2sc into next st, 2sc) around, ss to join rnd. *24sc*

Rnd 5: Ch 1, (work 2sc into next st, 3sc) around, ss to join rnd. *30sc*

Work one rnd even in sc without increasing.

Rnd 7: Ch 1, (work 2sc into next st, 4sc) around, ss to join rnd. *36sc*

Work one rnd even in sc without increasing.

Rnd 8: Ch 1, (work 2sc into next st, 5sc) around, ss to join rnd. *42sc*

Work one rnd even in sc without increasing.

Rnd 9: Ch 1, (work 2sc into next st, 6sc) around, ss to join rnd. *48sc*

Work nine rnds even in sc without increasing.

Begin to decrease as follows:

Rnd 19: Ch 1, (sc2tog, 6sc) around, ss to join rnd. *42sc*

Work one rnd even in sc without decreasing.

Rnd 21: Ch 1, (sc2tog, 5sc) around, ss to join rnd. *36sc*

Work one rnd even in sc without decreasing.

Rnd 23: Ch 1, (sc2tog, 4sc) around, ss to join rnd. *30sc*

Work one rnd even in sc without decreasing. Begin stuffing ball.

Rnd 25: Ch 1, (sc2tog, 3sc) around, ss to join rnd. *24sc*

Rnd 26: Ch 1, (sc2tog, 2sc) around, ss to join rnd. *18sc*

Rnd 27: Ch 1, (sc2tog, 1sc) around, ss to join rnd. *12sc*

Rnd 28: Decrease (sc2tog) evenly all round. *6sc*

Fasten off yarn.

FINISHING

Add more stuffing then sew up final hole to secure.

Then the babies were born, for the
where they slept in a bright
Babar and Celeste were congratulated by
each of whom bought a Pea

Chapter 6

Amigurumi Toys

 **Intermediate**

Bear

The embellishment, ears, and face of this adorable bear can all be easily changed to make other very sweet animals.

MEASUREMENTS
One size, approx 9¾in (25cm) tall.

YARN
1 x 1¾oz (50g) ball—approx 120yds (112m)—of Artesano Soft Merino Superwash DK, 100% merino superwash in each of:
Yarn A: shade 8413, baby peach
Yarn B: shade 7254, sand yellow

ALTERNATIVE YARNS
Any DK or light worsted weight yarn will do here to achieve the same size bear, although you could use any weight of yarn and the toy will simply come out a different size.

GAUGE (TENSION)
Exact gauge isn't essential for this project but make sure that you crochet tightly so that the stuffing does not show.

NOTIONS
*Size E/4 (3.5mm) crochet hook
*Stitch marker
*Darning needle
*Toy stuffing
*Two buttons for eyes

PATTERN NOTES
Pieces worked in the round, do not turn throughout. Rounds worked in spirals—do not join rounds except for body. Place a marker in first stitch of round to mark beginning of rounds and count rounds, move marker up every round.

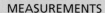

HEAD AND BODY
Using size E/4 (3.5mm) hook and yarn A, ch 2.

Rnd 1: Work 6sc into first ch made. Do not join rnd.

Rnd 2: Work 2sc into each sc around. *12sc*

Rnd 3: (Work 2sc into next st, 1sc) around. *18sc*

Rnd 4: (Work 2sc into next st, 2sc) around. *24sc*

Rnd 5: (Work 2sc into next st, 3sc) around. *30sc*

Rnd 6: (Work 2sc into next st, 4sc) around. *36sc*

Work one rnd even in sc without increasing.

Rnd 8: (Work 2sc into next st, 5sc) around. *42sc*

Work one rnd even in sc without increasing.

Rnd 10: (Work 2sc into next st, 6sc) around. *48sc*

Work one rnd even in sc without increasing.

Rnd 12: (Work 2sc into next st, 7sc) around. *54sc*

Work one rnd even in sc without increasing.

Rnd 14: (Work 2sc into next st, 8sc) around. *60sc*

Work eight rnds even in sc without increasing.

Begin to decrease as follows:

Rnd 23: (Sc2tog, 8sc) around. *54sc*

Work one rnd even in sc without decreasing.

Rnd 25: (Sc2tog, 7sc) around. *48sc*

Work one rnd even in sc without decreasing.

Rnd 27: (Sc2tog, 6sc) around. *42sc*

Work one rnd even in sc without decreasing.

Rnd 29: (Sc2tog, 5sc) around. *36sc*

Work one rnd even in sc without decreasing.

Rnd 31: (Sc2tog, 4sc) around. *30sc*

Rnd 32: (Sc2tog, 3sc) around. *24sc*

Stuff head fully.

Work one rnd even in sc without decreasing, join rnd with a ss.

Begin to work in separate rounds, joining at the end of each.

Rnd 34: Ch 1 (work 2sc into next st, 3sc) around, join rnd with a ss. *30sc*

Change to yarn B.

Rnd 35: Work even in sc without increasing, join rnd with a ss.

Change to yarn A.

Rnd 36: Ch 1, (work 2sc into next st, 4sc) around. *36sc*

Work one rnd even in sc without decreasing, join rnd with a ss.

Change to yarn B and work 2 rnds even in sc.

Cont even in sc, working 2-row stripes alternately of yarns A and B until body measures approx 2¼in (5.5cm).

Stuff body, ensuring enough stuffing is inserted to prevent head from drooping.

Begin to decrease, continuing in 2-row stripes alternately of yarns A and B, continuing to stuff body as necessary.

Next rnd: (Sc2tog, 4sc) around. *30sc*

Next rnd: (Sc2tog, 3sc) around. *24sc*

Next rnd: (Sc2tog, 2sc) around. *18sc*

Next rnd: (Sc2tog, 1sc) around. *12sc*

Next rnd: (Sc2tog) around. *6sc*

Fasten off yarn and sew up final hole to secure.

LEG

(make two)

Using size E/4 (3.5mm) hook and yarn A, ch 2.

Rnd 1: Work 5sc into first ch made. Do not join rnd, but work in spirals.

Rnds 2–3: Work 2sc into each sc around. *20sc*

Change to yarn B and work even in sc for eight rnds.

Stuff leg.

Next rnd: (Sc2tog) around. *10sc*

Work even in sc for two rnds, continuing to stuff leg as necessary.

Decrease around until you cannot decrease any more.

Fasten off yarn and sew up final hole to secure.

ARM

(make two)

Using size E/4 (3.5mm) hook and yarn A, ch 2.

Rnd 1: Work 5sc into first ch made, do not join rnd, but work in spirals.

Rnds 2–3: Work 2sc into each sc around. *20sc*

Change to yarn B and work even in sc for five rnds.

Stuff arm.

Decrease around until you cannot decrease any more.

Fasten off yarn and sew up final hole to secure.

EAR

(make two)

Using size E/4 (3.5mm) hook and yarn B, ch 2.

Row 1: Work 3sc into first ch made, turn.

Row 2: Ch 1, work 2sc into each sc around, turn. *6sc*

Row 3: Ch 1, (1sc, 2sc into next st) around, turn. *9sc*

Row 4: Ch 1, (2sc, 2sc into next st) around, turn. *12sc*

Row 4: Ch 1, (3sc, 2sc into next st) around, turn. *15sc*

Fasten off yarn.

FINISHING

Sew arms to sides of body and legs to bottom of body.

Sew ears to sides of head and sew on buttons for eyes and embroider a nose and smile on the face.

 **Intermediate**

Mushroom

A fun mushroom for decoration or to play with. Sewing on a face makes it into a cute creature.

MEASUREMENTS
Approx 4in (10cm) high.

YARN
1 x 1¾oz (50g) ball—approx 81yds (75m)—Sirdar Click Chunky with wool, 70% acrylic, 30% wool, in each of:
Yarn A: shade 142, lamb
Yarn B: shade 163, really red

ALTERNATIVE YARNS
Any chunky yarn will do to achieve the same size mushroom, although you could use any weight of yarn and the toy will simply come out a different size.

GAUGE (TENSION)
Exact gauge isn't essential for this project but make sure that you crochet tightly so that the stuffing does not show.

NOTIONS
∗Size H/8 (5mm) crochet hook
∗Stitch marker
∗Darning needle
∗Toy stuffing
∗Buttons for decoration
∗Scraps of yarn for embroidery

PATTERN NOTES
Mushroom is worked in the round, do not turn throughout. Rounds worked in spirals—do not join rounds. Place a marker in first stitch of round to mark beginning of rounds and count rounds, moving marker up every round.

MUSHROOM
Using size H/8 (5mm) hook and yarn A, ch 2.

Rnd 1: Work 6sc into first ch made, do not join rnd.

Rnd 2: Work 2sc into each sc around. *12sc*

Rnd 3: (Work 2sc into next st, 1sc) around. *18sc*

Rnd 4: (Work 2sc into next st, 2sc) around. *24sc*

Rnd 5: (Work 2sc into next st, 3sc) around. *30sc*

Work 1 rnd even in sc(blo), join rnd with a ss.

Work even in sc for five more rnds, in spirals, do not join rnds.

Next row: (3sc, sc2tog) around. *24sc*

Work one row even in sc.

Next row: (2sc, sc2tog) around. *18sc*

Fasten off yarn A, join in yarn B.

Stuff base of mushroom before crocheting cap.

Work one row even in sc.

Next row: Work 2sc into each sc around. *36sc*

Next row: (Work 2sc into next st, 1sc) around. *54sc*

Work three rows even in sc(blo).

Begin to decrease as folls:

Row 1: (4sc, sc2tog) around. *45sc*

Work 1 row even in sc. Begin to stuff cap.

Row 3: (3sc, sc2tog) around. *36sc*

Row 4: (2sc, sc2tog) around. *27sc*

Row 5: (Sc, sc2tog) around. *18sc*

Sc2tog around until hole closed.

Fasten off yarn and stitch rem hole closed.

FINISHING

Sew buttons (or beads) to cap for spots.

Embroider a simple face on the stalk of the mushroom.

 **Intermediate**

Frog

Who can resist this eager and easy frog with bulging eyes, a wide smile, and oversized feet?

MEASUREMENTS
One size, approx 4¾in (12cm) in height.

YARN
1 x 1¾oz (50g) ball—approx 137yds (125m)—Millamia Merino, 100% merino, in each of:
Yarn A: shade 141, grass
Yarn B: shade 142, daisy yellow

ALTERNATIVE YARNS
Any 4ply or sportweight yarn will do to achieve the same size frog, although you could use any weight of yarn and the toy will simply come out a different size.

GAUGE (TENSION)
Exact gauge isn't essential for this project but make sure that you crochet tightly so that the stuffing does not show.

NOTIONS
*Size D/3 (3.25mm) crochet hook
*Stitch marker
*Toy stuffing
*Felt for feet
*Darning needle
*Sewing needle and thread

PATTERN NOTES
Body and head are worked in the round, do not turn throughout. Rounds worked in spirals—do not join rounds unless instructed to. Place a marker in first stitch of round to mark beginning of rounds and count rounds, moving marker up every round. Begin from top of head.

HEAD AND BODY
Using size D/3 (3.25mm) hook and yarn A, ch 2.

Rnd 1: Work 6sc into first ch made, do not join rnd.

Rnd 2: Work 2sc into each sc around. *12sc*

Rnd 3: (Work 2sc into next st, 1sc) around. *18sc*

Rnd 4: (Work 2sc into next st, 2sc) around. *24sc*

Rnd 5: (Work 2sc into next st, 3sc) around. *30sc*

Rnd 6: (Work 2sc into next st, 4sc) around. *36sc*

Rnd 7: (Work 2sc into next st, 5sc) around. *42sc*

Work 1 rnd even in sc.

Rnd 9: (Work 2sc into next st, 6sc) around. *48sc*

Work 1 rnd even in sc.

Rnd 11: (Work 2sc into next st, 7sc) around. *54sc*

Work 1 rnd even in sc.

Rnd 13: (Work 2sc into next st, 8sc) around. *60sc*

Work 6 rows even in sc.

Begin to decrease as follows:

Rnd 20: (Sc2tog, 8sc) around, join rnd with a ss. *54sc*

Work 1 rnd even in sc.

Rnd 22: (Sc2tog, 7sc) around, join rnd with a ss. *48sc*

Work 1 rnd even in sc.

Rnd 24: (Sc2tog, 6sc) around, join rnd with a ss. *42sc*

Work 1 rnd even in sc.

Rnd 26: (Sc2tog, 5sc) around, join rnd with a ss. *36sc*

Rnd 27: (Sc2tog, 4sc) around, join rnd with a ss. *30sc*

Work four rnds even. Begin to stuff head from now.

Rnd 32: (Work 2sc into next st, 4sc) around. *36sc*

Rnd 33: (Work 2sc into next st, 5sc) around. *42sc*

Work four rnds even.

Rnd 38: (Sc2tog, 5sc) around, join rnd with a ss. *36sc*

Rnd 39: (Sc2tog, 4sc) around, join rnd with a ss. *30sc*

Stuff body.

Work 1 rnd even in sc, then 1 rnd even in sc(blo).

Rnd 42: (Sc2tog, 3sc) around, join rnd with a ss. *24sc*

Rnd 43: (Sc2tog, 2sc) around, join rnd with a ss. *18sc*

Rnd 44: (Sc2tog, 1sc) around, join rnd with a ss. *12sc*

Rnd 45: (Sc2tog) around, join rnd with a ss. *6sc*

Fasten off yarn and sew up any hole left.

EYE

(make two)

Using size D/3 (3.25mm) hook and yarn A, ch 2.

Rnd 1: Work 6sc into first ch made, do not join rnd.

Rnd 2: Work 2sc into each sc around. *12sc*

Rnd 3: (Work 2sc into next st, 1sc) around. *18sc*

Change to yarn B and work 2 rnds even in sc.

Rnd 6: (Sc2tog, 1sc) around, join rnd with a ss. *12sc*

Stuff eye.

Rnd 7: (Sc2tog) around, join rnd with a ss. *6sc*

Fasten off yarn and sew up any hole left.

TUMMY

Using size D/3 (3.25mm) hook and yarn B, ch 2.

Rnd 1: Work 6sc into first ch made, do not join rnd.

Rnd 2: Work 2sc into each sc around. *12sc*

Rnd 3: (Work 2sc into next st, 1sc) around. *18sc*

Rnd 4: (Work 2sc into next st, 2sc) around. *24sc*

Rnd 5: (Work 2sc into next st, 3sc) around. *30sc*

Fasten off yarn.

FINISHING

Sew eyes to top of head and tummy to body.

Embroider face with yarn B.

Cut out some webbed feet from the felt and sew to bottom of body.

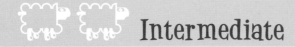 **Intermediate**

Penguin

This perky penguin is just calling to have his tummy squished! Why not try making him a scarf to keep him warm at the South Pole?

MEASUREMENTS
One size, approx 5½in (14cm) tall.

YARN
1 x 1¾oz (50g) ball—approx 137yds (125m)—Millamia Merino, 100% merino, in each of:
Yarn A: shade 101, midnight navy
Yarn B: shade 142, daisy yellow
Yarn C: shade 124, snow white

ALTERNATIVE YARNS
Any 4ply or sportweight yarn will do here to achieve the same size penguin, although you could use any weight of yarn and the toy will simply come out a different size. The embellishments use very little yarn, so you can use scraps from other projects.

GAUGE (TENSION)
Exact gauge isn't essential for this project but make sure that you crochet tightly so that the stuffing does not show.

NOTIONS
*Size D/3 (3.25mm) crochet hook
*Stitch marker
*Darning needle
*Toy stuffing
*Buttons for eyes

PATTERN NOTES
Pieces are worked flat and the body and beak are worked in the round, do not turn throughout. Rounds worked in spirals—do not join rounds. Place a marker in first stitch of round to mark beginning of rounds and count rounds, moving marker up every round.

HEAD AND BODY
Using size D/3 (3.25mm) crochet hook and yarn A, ch 2.

Rnd 1: Work 7sc into first ch made, do not join rnd.

Rnd 2: Work 2sc into each sc around. *14sc*

Rnd 3: (Work 2sc into next st, 1sc) around. *21sc*

Rnd 4: (Work 2sc into next st, 2sc) around. *28sc*

Rnd 5: (Work 2sc into next st, 3sc) around. *35sc*

Work five rnds even in sc without increasing.

Begin to decrease as follows:

Rnd 11: (Sc2tog, 3sc) around. *28sc*

Rnd 12: (Sc2tog, 2sc) around. *21sc*

Stuff head fully.

Work two rnds even in sc without decreasing.

Rnd 15: (Work 2sc into next st, 2sc) around. *28sc*

Rnd 16: (Work 2sc into next st, 3sc) around. *35sc*

Rnd 17: (Work 2sc into next st, 4sc) around. *42sc*

Work one rnd even in sc without increasing.

Rnd 19: (Work 2sc into next st, 5sc) around. *49sc*

Work one rnd even in sc without increasing.

Rnd 21: (Work 2sc into next st, 6sc) around. *56sc*

Work one rnd even in sc without increasing.

Rnd 22: (Work 2sc into next st, 7sc) around. *63sc*

Work three rnds even in sc without increasing.

Begin to decrease, as follows:

Rnd 26: (Sc2tog, 7sc) around. *56sc*

Work one rnd even in sc without decreasing.

Rnd 28: (Sc2tog, 6sc) around. *49sc*

Work one rnd even in sc without decreasing.

Rnd 30: (Sc2tog, 5sc) around. *42sc*

Work one rnd even in sc without decreasing. Begin to stuff body.

Rnd 32: (Sc2tog, 4sc) around. *35sc*

Rnd 33: (Sc2tog, 3sc) around. *28sc*

Rnd 34: (Sc2tog, 2sc) around. *21sc*

Rnd 35: (Sc2tog, 1sc) around. *14sc*

Rnd 36: (Sc2tog) around. *7sc*

Fasten off yarn and sew up final hole to secure.

FOOT

(make two)

Using size D/3 (3.25mm) crochet hook and yarn B, ch 4.

Row 1: Work 1sc into 2nd ch from hook, sc into each ch to end, turn. *3sc*

Row 2: Ch 1, work 2sc into first st, sc, 2sc into last st, turn. *5sc*

Row 3: Ch 1, sc to end of row, turn.

Row 4: Ch 1, work 2sc into first st, sc, 2sc into last st, turn. *7sc*

Row 5: Ch 1, sc to end of row.

Fasten off yarn.

WING

(make two)

Using size D/3 (3.25mm) crochet hook and yarn A, ch 3.

Row 1: Work 1 sc into 2nd ch from hook, sc into next chain, turn. *2sc*

Row 2: Ch 1, work 2sc into first st, 2sc into last st, turn. *4sc*

Row 3: Ch 1, work 2sc into first st, 2sc, 2sc into last st, turn. *6sc*

Row 4-6: Ch 1, sc to end of row, turn.

Fasten off yarn.

BEAK

Using size D/3 (3.25mm) crochet hook and yarn B, ch 3.

Work in the round in spirals.

Rnd 1: Work 5sc into 2nd ch from hook, do not turn.

Work 1 rnd even.

Rnd 3: Work 2sc into each sc around. *10sc*

Fasten off yarn.

TUMMY

Using size D/3 (3.25mm) crochet hook and yarn C, ch 2.

Work in the round in spirals.

Rnd 1: Work 6sc into 2nd ch from hook, do not turn.

Rnd 2: Work 2sc into each sc around. *12sc*

Rnd 3: Work (1sc, 2sc into next st) around. *18sc*

Rnd 4: 3sc, 3dc, 6sc, 3dc, sc to end of rnd, join with a ss to first sc.

Fasten off yarn.

FINISHING

Sew wings to sides of body and feet to bottom of body.

Sew white oval to penguin's tummy.

Sew on buttons for eyes and sew on beak.

Advanced

Dinosaur

A cute and cuddly dinosaur, which can be easily adapted to become a scary, growling version!

MEASUREMENTS
One size, approx 5in (13cm) tall.

YARN
1 x 1¾oz (50g) ball—approx 191yds (175m)—Sirdar Snuggly Kisses DK, 55% nylon, 45% acrylic, in each of:
Yarn A: shade 750, hushed
Yarn B: shade 760, sunshine

ALTERNATIVE YARNS
Any DK or light worsted weight yarn will work well for this project.

GAUGE (TENSION)
Exact gauge isn't essential for this project but make sure that you crochet tightly so that the stuffing does not show.

NOTIONS
*Size D/3 (3.25mm) and size E/4 (3.5mm) crochet hooks
*Darning needle
*Sewing needle and thread
*Toy stuffing
*Felt for claws
*Two buttons for eyes
*Oddments of yarn for embellishment

PATTERN NOTES
The body and head are worked in rounds—join with a ss and do not turn. The tail is worked in the round in spirals—do not turn and and do not join rounds. Place a marker in first stitch of round to mark beginning of rounds and count rounds, moving marker up every round.

BODY AND HEAD
Using size D/3 (3.25mm) hook and yarn A, ch 2.

Rnd 1: Work 6sc into first ch made, join rnd with a ss.

Rnd 2: Work 2sc into each sc around, join rnd with a ss. *12sc*

Rnd 3: (Work 2sc into next st, 1sc) around, join rnd with a ss. *18sc*

Rnd 4: (Work 2sc into next st, 2sc) around, join rnd with a ss. *24sc*

Rnd 5: (Work 2sc into next st, 3sc) around, join rnd with a ss. *30sc*

Rnd 6: (Work 2sc into next st, 4sc) around, join rnd with a ss. *36sc*

Rnd 7: (Work 2sc into next st, 5sc) around, join rnd with a ss. *42sc*

Rnd 8: (Work 2sc into next st, 6sc) around, join rnd with a ss. *48sc*

Work seven rnds even in sc without increasing.

Stuff body.

Begin to decrease as follows:

Rnd 16: (Sc2tog, 6sc) around, join rnd with a ss. *42sc*

Work one rnd even without decreasing.

Rnd 18: (Sc2tog, 5sc) around, join rnd with a ss. *36sc*

Work one rnd even without decreasing.

Rnd 20: (Sc2tog, 4sc) around, join rnd with a ss. *30sc*

Work nine rnds even without decreasing.

Rnd 30: (Sc2tog, 3sc) around, join rnd with a ss. *24sc*

Work one rnd even without decreasing.

Begin to stuff head from now.

Rnd 31: (Sc2tog, 2sc) around, join rnd with a ss. *18sc*

Rnd 32: (Sc2tog, 1sc) around, join rnd with a ss. *12sc*

Rnd 33: (Sc2tog) around, join rnd with a ss. *6sc*

Fasten off yarn. Sew up final hole to secure.

TAIL
Using size D/3 (3.25mm) hook and yarn A, ch 12 and join into a ring with a ss into first ch.

Rnd 1: Sc into each ch around, do not join rnd.

Rnd 2: Sc into each st around, do not join rnd.

Rep last rnd until tail measures approx 1in (2.5cm).

Next rnd: (Sc2tog) around. *6sc*

Work two more rows on these 6 sts, then fasten off yarn and sew up final hole to secure.

BACK SCALES
(worked straight)

Using size E/4 (3.5mm) hook and yarn B, ch 34.

Row 1: Work 1sc into 2nd ch from hook, then into each ch to end, turn. *33sc*

Row 2: Ch 1, (skip 1sc, 5dc into next sc, skip 1sc, sc into next st) to end of row.

Fasten off yarn.

FINISHING

Stuff tail and sew to dinosaur's bottom.

Sew back scales down the back of dinosaur's head and back, covering the joining stitches, and onto his tail.

Sew on buttons onto head for eyes, then embroider a mouth and teeth using oddments of yarn.

Cut claws out of felt and sew to bottom of body for feet and over tummy for hands.

Advanced

Kitty Cat

A cute little tabby kitten that can be made to match your own moggie by working it in different colors, such as black and white for a tuxedo cat.

MEASUREMENTS
One size, cat is approx 6in (15cm) long.

YARN
1 x 1¾oz (50g) ball—approx 104yds (95m)—Sirdar Snuggly Baby Bamboo DK, 80% bamboo, 20% wool, in each of:
Yarn A: shade 128, tigger
Yarn B: shade 154, poppy
Yarn C: shade 134, babe (only very small amounts used, scraps of other yarns are fine to use here)

ALTERNATIVE YARNS
Any DK or light worsted weight yarn will make the same sized cat, but try other weights for different-sized toys.

GAUGE (TENSION)
Exact gauge isn't essential for this project but make sure that you crochet tightly so that the stuffing does not show.

NOTIONS
*Size D/3 (3.25mm) crochet hook
*Darning needle
*Sewing needle and thread
*Toy stuffing
*Felt for ears
*Two buttons for eyes
*Oddments of yarn for embellishment

PATTERN NOTES
Pieces are worked in the round, do not turn throughout. Head and body are worked in completed rounds. Arms, legs and tail are worked in spirals—for these, do not join rounds. Place a marker in first stitch of round to mark beginning of rounds and count rounds, moving marker up every round.

HEAD
Using size D/3 (3.25mm) hook and yarn A, ch 2.

Rnd 1: Work 6sc into first ch made, join rnd with a ss.

Rnd 2: Work 2sc into each sc around, join rnd with a ss. *12sc*

Rnd 3: (Work 2sc into next st, 1sc) around, join rnd with a ss. *18sc*
Change to yarn B.

Rnd 4: (Work 2sc into next st, 2sc) around, join rnd with a ss. *24sc*

Rnd 5: (Work 2sc into next st, 3sc) around, join rnd with a ss. *30sc*
Change to yarn A.

Rnd 6: (Work 2sc into next st, 4sc) around, join rnd with a ss. *36sc*

Work seven rnds even in sc without increasing, continuing in alternate 2-row stripes of yarns A and B.

Begin to decrease, continuing to work in stripes as established, as follows:

Rnd 14: (Sc2tog, 4sc) around, join rnd with a ss. *30sc*

Rnd 15: (Sc2tog, 3sc) around, join rnd with a ss. *24sc*
Begin to stuff head from now.

Rnd 16: (Sc2tog, 2sc) around, join rnd with a ss. *18sc*

Rnd 17: (Sc2tog, 1sc) around, join rnd with a ss. *12sc*

Rnd 18: (Sc2tog) around, join rnd with a ss. *6sc*
Fasten off yarn and sew up final hole to secure.

BODY

Using size D/3 (3.25mm) hook and Yarn A, ch 2.

Rnd 1: Work 6sc into first ch made, join rnd with a ss.

Rnd 2: Work 2sc into each sc around, join rnd with a ss. *12sc*

Rnd 3: (Work 2sc into next st, 1sc) around, join rnd with a ss. *18sc*

Change to yarn B.

Rnd 4: (Work 2sc into next st, 2sc) around, join rnd with a ss. *24sc*

Rnd 5: (Work 2sc into next st, 3sc) around, join rnd with a ss. *30sc*

Change to yarn A.

Rnd 6: (Work 2sc into next st, 4sc) around, join rnd with a ss. *36sc*

Rnd 7: (Work 2sc into next st, 5sc) around, join rnd with a ss. *42sc*

Change to yarn B.

Rnd 8: (Work 2sc into next st, 6sc) around, join rnd with a ss. *48sc*

Work eight rnds even in sc without increasing, continuing in alternate 2-row stripes of yarns A and B.

Begin to decrease, continuing to work in stripes as established, as follows:

Rnd 17: (Sc2tog, 6sc) around, join rnd with a ss. *42sc*

Rnd 18: (Sc2tog, 5sc) around, join rnd with a ss. *36sc*

Rnd 19: (Sc2tog, 4sc) around, join rnd with a ss. *30sc*

Rnd 20: (Sc2tog, 3sc) around, join rnd with a ss. *24sc*

Begin to stuff head from now.

Rnd 21: (Sc2tog, 2sc) around, join rnd with a ss. *18sc*

Rnd 22: (Sc2tog, 1sc) around, join rnd with a ss. *12sc*

Rnd 23: (Sc2tog) around, join rnd with a ss. *6sc*

Fasten off yarn and sew up final hole to secure.

ARM

(make two)

Using size D/3 (3.25mm) hook and yarn A, ch 2.

Rnd 1: Work 5sc into first ch made. Do not join rnd.

Work even in sc in spirals on these 5 sts until arm is approx ¾in (2cm) long.

Fasten off yarn.

LEG

(make two)

Using size D/3 (3.25mm) hook and yarn A, ch 2.

Rnd 1: Work 5sc into first ch made. Do not join rnd.

Work even in sc in spirals on these 5 sts until leg is approx 1in (2.5cm) long.

Fasten off yarn.

TAIL

Using size D/3 (3.25mm) hook and yarn A, ch 2.

Rnd 1: Work 5sc into first ch made. Do not join rnd.

Work even in sc in spirals on these 5 sts until tail is approx 3in (8cm) long.

Fasten off yarn.

NOSE

Using size D/3 (3.25mm) hook and yarn C, ch 2.

Rnd 1: Work 6sc into first ch made, join rnd with a ss.

Rnd 2: Work 2sc into each sc around, join rnd with a ss. *12sc*

Fasten off yarn.

FINISHING

Sew head to body, with first rnds you made facing front, so that stripes appear as circles on the face and tummy. Sew arms to body, just below neck. Sew legs to bottom of body. Sew on tail at back of body.

Sew nose circle to front of face and embroider nose, mouth, and whiskers with simple straight stitches. Sew on buttons for eyes. Cut out felt ears and sew to top of head.

Abbreviations

US TERMS

beg = beginning
blo = back loop only
ch = chain
dec = decrease
dc = double crochet
dc2tog = double crochet 2 together – a decrease of 1 st
hdc = half double crochet
inc = increase
pm = place marker
rem = remaining
rep = repeat
rnd = round
sc = single crochet
sc2tog = single crochet 2 together – a decrease of 1 stitch
sk = skip – skip indicated number of stitches
sp(s) = space(s)
ss = slip stitch
st(s) = stitch(es)
tbl = through back loop
tog = together

US TO UK TERMS

US = UK
dc = tr
hdc = htr
gauge = tension
sc = dc
skip = miss
ss = sl st

HOOK SIZE CONVERSION TABLE

US hook	Metric (mm)	Old UK hook
-	2.0	14
B/1	2.25	13
-	2.5	12
C/2	2.75	-
-	3.0	11
D/3	3.25	10
E/4	3.5	9
F/5	3.75	-
G/6	4.0	8
7	4.5	7
H/8	5.0	6
I/9	5.5	5
J/10	6.0	4
K/10.5	6.5	3
-	7.0	2
-	7.5	-
L/11	8.0	0
M/13	9.0	00
N/15	10.0	000

Suppliers

USA

DEBBIE BLISS
SIRDAR
Knitting Fever Inc.
PO Box 336
315 Bayview Ave
Amityville, NY 11701
Tel: (516) 546-3600
Fax: (516) 546-6871
www.knittingfever.com

ROWAN YARNS
REGIA
Westminster Fibers Inc.
4 Townsend West
Suite 8
Nashua
NH 03063
Tel: (063) 886-5041
www.westminsterfibers.com

PATONS
Coats & Clark
Consumer Services
P.O. Box 12229
Greenville
SC 29612-0229
Tel: (800) 648-1479
www.coatsandclark.com

THE DMC CORPORATION
10 Basin Drive, Suite 130
Kearny, NJ 07032
Tel: 9-5pm EST M-Th, 9-2:30 F
(973) 589-0606
www.dmc-usa.com

PURL (SHOP)
459 Broome Street
New York
NY 10013
Tel: (212) 420-8796
www.purlsoho.com

DOWNTOWN YARNS (SHOP)
45 Avenue A
New York
NY 10009
Tel: (212) 995-5991
www.downtownyarns.com

Canada

PATONS
320 Livingstone Avenue South
Listowel
Ontario N4W 3H3
Tel: 1-888-368-8401
www.patonsyarns.com

DEBBIE BLISS
REGIA
ROWAN YARNS
SIRDAR
Diamond Yarns Ltd
155 Martin Ross Avenue
Unit 3
Toronto
Ontario M3J 2L9
Tel: 416-736-6111
www.diamondyarn.com

DMC
H.A. Kidd
5 Northline Road
Toronto
Canada M4B 3P2
Tel: 416-364-6451
Fax: 416-364-5733
www.hakidd.com

UK

SIRDAR SPINNING LTD.
Flanshaw Lane
Wakefield
West Yorkshire WF2 9ND
United Kingdom
Tel: 01924 231 669
Email: orders@sirdar.co.uk

DEBBIE BLISS
Designer Yarns
Unit 8-10 Newbridge Industrial Estate
Pitt Street
Keighley
West Yorkshire BD21 4PQ
Tel: 01535 664222
Fax: 01535 664333
www.designeryarns.uk.com

ROWAN YARNS
Green Lane Mill
Holmfirth
West Yorkshire HD9 2DX
Tel: 01484 681881
www.knitrowan.com

PATONS
Coats Crafts UK
PO Box 22
Lingfield House
Lingfield Point
McMullen Road
Darlington
County Durham DL1 1YQ
Tel: 01325 394237
www.coatscrafts.co.uk

DMC CREATIVE WORLD LTD
Unit 21, Warren Park Way
Warrens Park
Enderby
Leicester LE19 4SA
Tel: 0116 2754000
www.dmccreative.co.uk

CRYSTAL PALACE YARNS
Hantex Ltd
Unit 1 Whitehouse Business Units
Eaudyke
Friskney
Lincolnshire PE22 8NL
Tel 01754 820800
Fax 01754 820110
www.hantex.co.uk

ARTESANO LTD
Unit G, Lamb's Farm Business Park,
Basingstoke Rd
Swallowfield
Reading
Berkshire RG7 1PQ England
Tel: 0118 9503350
Email: jenny@artesanoyarns.co.uk
www.artesanoyarns.co.uk

Acknowledgments

MILLAMIA
Tel: 08450 17 74 74.
www.millamia.com

MRS MOON (SHOP)
41 Crown Road
St Margarets
Twickenham TW1 3EJ
Tel: 020 8744 1190
www.mrsmoon.co.uk

LOOP (SHOP)
15 Camden Passage, Islington,
London N1 8EA
Tel: 020 7288 1160
Email: info@loopknitting.com

NEST (SHOP)
102 Weston Park
Crouch End
London N8 9PP
Tel: 020 8340 8852
Email: info@handmadenest.co.uk
www.handmadenest.co.uk

International

RICO YARNS
RICO DESIGN GmbH & Co.
KG Industriestrasse 19 - 23
33034 Brakel
www.amc-design.de

I have wanted to write a crochet book for a very long time, and *Crochet for Children* was a great project to work on for my first book using this craft. I hugely enjoyed designing and making the projects, especially the toys, which are my favorite projects to work on. However, I could not have completed this without the help and support of a great team.

Firstly, I must thank the gorgeous and talented models—Aiden, Kiera, Emilee, Alice, Dominic, Daniella, Emily—who were great fun to work with and were so enthusiastic about the projects and the crafts they were photographed modeling and demonstrating. It is great for me as a craftsperson to see the joy that crafts can bring to a child, and to know that in this technological age they still have huge enthusiasm for such an ancient pastime.

Thanks again to the design team who yet again have created a beautiful and fun-looking book, which captures the essence of my designs perfectly. Martin and Emma, the photographers who have produced such joyful shots, Cindy, Pete, Sally, Emma, Tom, Sophie, Zoe, and especially Kate, for their support and organizational skills, which meant I only had to worry about creating pretty projects.

The companies who donated yarns have been fabulous, especially the lovely Millamia, Sirdar, Rico, and Cara and Kate at DMC, who have gone out of their way to help.

Finally, thanks to my family for putting up with me crocheting non-stop, even during Sunday lunches and card games. There is one person without whom I would not have been able to finish the book, the person who patiently taught and re-taught me how to crochet whenever I inconveniently fancied picking up the hook as a child, usually when she was busily working on a crocheted shawl. When granny squares were coming out of my ears, Mary stepped in to take the pressure off at a very trying time. So thanks for everything mum, and I am looking forward to my own crocheted shawl in the very near future.

Heartfelt thanks to you all.

Claire

Index